D0571706

THE WAYS OF NIHILISM

93394

QS
2387
W5
1970

THE
WAYS OF
NIHILISM

&

A STUDY OF
HERMAN MELVILLE'S
SHORT NOVELS

KINGSLEY WIDMER

DISCARDED

A PUBLICATION OF
THE CALIFORNIA STATE COLLEGES

For Matthew and Jonah;
may they go beyond . . . .

Copyright © 1970 by
The Board of Trustees of The California State Colleges.
Library of Congress Catalog Card Number 73-129222
Printed in the United States of America by
Anderson, Ritchie & Simon, Los Angeles
Designed by Joseph Simon

PREFACE

This study is partly indebted to some candid students who complained that my published articles on Melville lacked the breadth and the force of our classroom discussions. I have tried here to overcome some of that narrowness. But—as teacher-scholars, and talker-writers, ruefully know—the differences between immediate responsiveness and the formalities of scholarly criticism cannot so easily, or conveniently, be willed away. Yet we must try a larger reach.

In doing so, I chose to subordinate learning and critical technique to a more speculative and tendentious dialectic, though still based in an exacting literary analysis of the representative texts. I therefore redeveloped, instead of revising and reprinting, my earlier Melville studies. My thanks are due the editors who first accepted them in considerably different and shorter form: "The Negative Affirmation: Melville's *Bartleby*," *Modern Fiction Studies*, VIII (Autumn 1962); "The Perplexity of Melville: *Benito Cereno*," *Studies in Short Fiction*, V (Spring 1968); and "The Perplexed Myths of Melville: *Billy Budd*," *Novel: Forum on Fiction*, II (Fall 1968).

Gratitude of a different sort is due a number of Melville scholars, starting with those I first listened to as a student two decades ago. What they said, and left unsaid, drove me to a prolonged and perplexed involvement with Melville's writings. These essays are intended as a corrective of what I was taught in classroom and library. While academic decorum forbids a fully specific acknowledgment to the specialists in Melville, a larger debt should be visible. I have read most of the material on Melville, used what I could, and cited representative examples in the notes. Without such works there would not be the public occasion for my own approach, which suggests a proper regard for the community of scholars. I also equally appreciate the efforts of the three Melvilleans who served as "readers" of my manuscript—one flattering, one perplexed, and one outraged. For those students of Melville who may be offended by what they take to be contumacious criticism, I plead that lovely aphorism of Blake's, "Opposition is true friendship."

My concern here with the oppositional problems surrounding Melville's short novels owes something to my efforts in "non-literary" writing and other activity. In this direction, I would like to thank those who gave me opportunity to involve my studies of Melville in contemporary debate. At the invitation of Professor Kermit Vanderbilt, I included discussion of Melville scholarship in a criticism of the pseudo-objectivity of literary study given as the Luncheon Address to the American Literature Section of the Philological Association of the Pacific Coast (Tucson, November 30, 1968). Professor C. R. Webb invited me to discuss Melville and the problem of "blackness" in white American consciousness at a symposium sponsored by the California State Colleges and the University of California (Laguna Beach, February 7, 1969). In each portion of the following essay, I have continued the effort to suggest some of the contemporary social and other human pertinence of the literary experience. I do not understand how we dare do anything less.

I am grateful to the open and helpful ways of all those involved in the Faculty Publications Program of the California State Colleges. However, neither they, nor my students, editors, teachers and colleagues, should be held responsible for my practice of contentious *belles lettres*. As with my other books, my greatest difficulties have been with my most learned, astute, sensitive and devastating critic, Dr. Eleanor Widmer. And my greatest pleasures.

KINGSLEY WIDMER
San Diego State College

CONTENTS

THE WAYS OF NIHILISM

CHAPTER ONE

INTRODUCTION: BEYOND PERPLEXITY?

Academic literary study can serve, I hope, some variety of purpose. Or at least it need not entirely confine itself to the utilities and rituals of institutional culture.[1] To go beyond treating the literary work as an honorific and mortuary artifact means to meditate about it with less than usual academic piety. Literature then provides a nexus for considering anguished human problems. It takes some such purpose to make scholarly criticism a serious intellectual engagement. Perhaps the problem of justifying literary study is mostly a practical one: criticism is as criticism does. If it reaches real issues with perception and rigor and vitality, it needs no learned rationale. But if it does not, no method or manner will make it true criticism.

For this essay in criticism I have started with some conven-

[1]One incentive for this book, beyond my earlier studies of Melville, came from a discussion of the functions of academic literary criticism. I proposed some of its dimensions in "The Literary Institutionalization of D. H. Lawrence: An Anti-Review of the Current State of Lawrence Studies," *Paunch, A Journal of Romanticism*, 26 (April 1966). This elicited several counter-statements from Professor Mark Spilka *(The Love-Ethic of D. H. Lawrence)*, and the editor, Professor Arthur Efron, which, with my rebuttal, were published as "Controversy," *Paunch*, 27 (October 1966). Some of the discussion focused on interpretations of Melville. Efron's argument was expanded in "Criticism and Literature in the One-Dimensional Age," *Minnesota Review*, VIII (Winter 1968). Spilka's view became part of the editorial policy of a journal, *Novel: Forum on Fiction*. My further arguments appeared in various books and articles, a few of which will be cited below.

tional assumptions but with the hope of reaching beyond them. With a minimum of institutional and self-interested motives, we might pose the simple but basic critical questions. What literary works shall we meditate upon? For oppositional reasons, let us try some of the most recognized and discussed writings in orthodox American culture. What human problems shall we, with passionate disinterest, pursue? The most perplexed ones relatable to the literature. Why else bother? What limits shall we set, what meditative discipline? Again, I have chosen obvious ones—what has been for a generation of literary scholars the widely practiced "close reading" of some perplexed "classics," an explication of Melville's short novels.

As the quotes suggest, I recognize serious limitations to both the analytic methods of interpretive explication and to the canonical-pedagogical selection of materials. But here I shall not argue those issues. Melville's "short novels"—most everyone admits the designation to be somewhat vague and arbitrary yet nonetheless conventionally useful—bear a considerable burden of scholarship and criticism. The dangers in taking it up must now include temptations to ingeniousness and to contentiousness. Knowing much of what has been said and written about these works makes such responses unavoidable. They can be modulated, and that I have tried to do, but hardly denied, and so I grant these critical vices. Like most vices, they can take some salutary as well as indulgent ways. Again, I shall not argue the issue but only note, like Augustine of Hippo, that from these vices the critic may hope to be saved, but not too soon—not, anyway, until his next book.

My lesser ingenuities include taking three literary works much discussed separately and putting them together. Surprisingly, few critics analyze *Bartleby, Benito Cereno* and *Billy Budd* as closely related.[2] Apparent reasons for this include differences in scene—

---

[2]Stanley Edgar Hyman is one of the very few to have noticed the parallelism of the three novellas. "Melville the Scrivener," *New Mexico Quarterly*, XXIII (Winter 1953), p. 407.

a New York office, ships off the South American coast, a British frigate at sea during the French Revolution—as well as disparities in the time of writing. *Billy Budd* seems not to be considered with the other two because not directly American in material and written a generation later. Other differences could, and will, be noted, including contrasts in sources and styles and emphases in the three short novels. Yet, as the titles suggest, these are parallel prose narratives, the only three works of Melville's of such intermediate length. Important thematic similarities, I believe, also fully justify discussing them together. More than with a single work yet less tediously than with the whole body of Melville's writing, they provide opportunities to discuss a still significant attitude.[3]

Another debatable ingenuity came upon me long after writing my original discussions. I have reversed the chronological order of the short novels. As in social morality, there is always much good reason for putting the last first. Even if the new ordering be as arbitrary as the old, in its newness it at least has the considerable advantage of shifting the injustice. I find many of the discussions of *Billy Budd* canted, understandably, by the work's position as a final "testament" of the author. An established biographical as well as chronological pattern tends to determine the reading of the story. Putting *Billy Budd* first and Melville's first short fiction, *Bartleby*, last, then, aims to be corrective. The counter-order furthers, hopefully, some counter-arguments. Since I hold that *Bartleby* is the most aesthetically and morally successful of Melville's works, far more so than *Billy Budd*, there is at least that appropriateness to the arrangement. Furthermore, I want to suggest that *Bartleby* answers some of the perplexities of *Billy Budd*—an ethic of resistance reaches beyond despair.

Is it fair to use one of an author's works to answer another?

[3]Here I gratefully follow the arguments of a number of reviewers of my first book, *The Art of Perversity: D. H. Lawrence's Shorter Fictions* (Seattle, Wash., 1962), which relentlessly discussed all the stories.

This is certainly assumed in the arguments which see *Billy Budd* as a "testament" or penultimate statement. That view as well as mine supposes a continuity of mind and an inter-relatedness of Melville's works which it would be difficult to fully justify even though one finds no substantial argument for a transformation between "middle" and "late" Melville. It is, of course, to the convenience of criticism not to grant a fragmentation of the authorial mind. That would be reductive and atomizing of the works. But even if there were no unified authorial mind behind the literature—contrary to the usual assumption which makes "Melvilleanism" the actual (though not always admitted) subject of study—we could still struggle to see a continuity of concern and response in which one work does answer another. Those are the dialectics which make culture.

There is, of course, little justification for assuming that the last in a sequence—sometimes called "the wisdom of age"—provides the more pertinent answers. Since I shall argue that these tales constitute an attack on the legitimacy of all authority, my sequence of discussion might reasonably reflect my argument. Standard chronology, like any youth-to-age pattern, tends to falsify perception. And it certainly encourages specious claims to moral and cultural authority.

Does all this sound as if explication and interpretation has become a speculative realm? Necessarily, I am arguing that literary criticism journey into such lands. These three tales provide appropriate landscapes for such intellectual travels. Each of these stories centers on a figure of authority and his victim, a sacrificial image of human pathos for whom the story is named—Billy Budd, Benito Cereno, Bartleby. The recurrent pattern insists on the peculiarities of the Melvillean world, on human isolation amidst hostile forces in a dubious order marked by riddling incommunication and lack of solace. Incomprehension and resentment encourage the malicious. Each story turns about an ambiguous rebellion against or refusal of such a world. Melville's ruminative style, which leads to the merely garrulous in some of his writing, here heightens by contrast, and enlarges by acceptance, the ominous relevance of such isolation and extremity. Melville treats the victims with a curiously mixed attitude which includes both a fervor of apotheosis and a Pyrrhic mockery. They are simultaneously exploited innocents and incurable self-destroyers. The fusion expresses a bitter view of what happens to innocence in this world. Such forlornness, to use a favorite word of Melville's, certainly grounds itself in despair, in a loss of hope in the possibilities of goodness and in a harsh view of what passes for virtue and order.

The figures of authority in these short novels—Captain Vere, Captain Delano, and Bartleby's unnamed attorney—seem eminently sensible, kindly, virtuous, and even superior and heroic. Yet one way and another they are patently obtuse, condemn the innocent to death, and embody a repressive and illegitimate order. The authority figures' most elaborate self-rationalizations—the main material of the stories, to an almost obsessive degree—seem woven with ironies as well as warped with inhumanities. For reasons which should become clear later, we must, I believe, reckon them as ideological representatives of a still dominant Western mode: let us call it "benevolent rationalism." Melville's perspective here is "illiberal"; whether the implications are finally "conservative" or "radical" provides an intriguing problem. As I see them, the tales perplex our whole sense of benevolent rationalism, ending in its denial. Thus they must be read not only as philosophical tales but as attacks on our prevalent views of order and legitimacy and authority.

Let me turn from this incomplete summary back to the function of criticism. My brief account, it might be said, already violates several principles of scholarly criticism, at least as some propound them.[4] My mode of abstraction is such as to combine description, explication, interpretation and evaluation. Otherwise put, this is a "loaded" description (even though a restrained

4For representative example, see E. D. Hirsch, Jr., *Validity in Interpretation* (New Haven, Conn., 1967).

one) with an "ideological line." It should, in my opinion, not be otherwise. How, in humanistic studies, did we ever pretend to such things as "neutral" descriptions, "objective" explications, "aesthetic" evaluations, and the rest of pseudo-scientific literary criticism? That description or explication of a work which appears to be "neutral" has either cleverly covered over the interpretations and judgments and implications which will be fished out of it later, or it has settled for the worst of all ideological positions, the reduction of meaning to a trivial puddle. Such pretenses also conveniently serve bad motives, the acquiesence not only in comfortably accepted interpretations and evaluations but subservience to prevailing institutional ideologies.

To refuse to be "neutral" in such fashion also means to refuse to segregate critical functions. Evaluation does not get added, like frosting to bread, after the accumulation of data and analysis. If the sweetness or sourness is not there at the start, it never really belongs. Or, to switch the metaphor, the analytic chore-work cannot be separated from the significance of any job since both are the job. To refuse to neutralize criticism, whether in manner or in division of labor, does not necessarily mean to be unjust or simple-minded or merely moralistic. To propound a view need not deny the subtle and complex and paradoxical and ambiguous, except as ends in themselves, which they never can truly be anyway. Sheer cleverness or erudition, of which there is considerable in the Melville scholarship, exploits the merits of play, but not much else. By what strange logic have we, from Aristotle on, pretended to a devalued universe of human discourse? That itself denies existing, mortal man as well as the value of his literature.

It is a commonplace to "objectively" insist on the perplexity of Melville's writings. It is true, but not true enough. Perhaps a brief example will clarify the issue. We may apply to Melville his own statement about truth in Shakespeare ("Hawthorne and His Mosses"): "in this world of lies, Truth is forced to fly like a scared white doe in the woodlands; and only by cunning glimpses will she reveal herself, as in Shakespeare and other masters of the great Art of Telling the truth—even though it be covertly and by snatches."[5] Curiously, there are several kinds of truth here. We cannot, unlike some scholars on Melville, ignore his insistent and encompassing *truth*—this is a "world of lies" which scares away the gentle and beautiful. Awareness of *that* is the major and conditioning truth for all others. Secondly, we have the forlorn pastoral image of the good—"a scared white doe in the woodlands"—which in one form or another recurs so often in Melville's writings. Third, we have the "great Art of Telling the truth," which depends on "cunning glimpses," though not itself that scared doe. To cunningly perceive and tell the flying white truths, we must recognize two other truths: the snatching covertness of the artist, and the whole dark wood of lies.

The point as well as manner here encourage some perplexity. But Melville's famed "ambiguities" should not be taken as merely literary techniques or endless moral riddlings. Ambiguity is never all, though Melville sometimes tempts his critics to that dark conclusion. Probably, those whitely positive and skittish truths of goodness and innocence are incomprehensible. As he says in *Pierre*, "a mysteriousness wholly hopeless of solution." As Melville's Pierre also cries, "I seem to founder in the perplexity."[6]

But the critic's duty is not to settle for the ambiguities and perplexities, not to founder there, either like a despairing incestuous adolescent or a scared white doe. Granted, at the most general level Melville did founder, and the much quoted Hawthorne description—"He can neither believe, nor be comfortable in his unbelief . . ."—seems apt not only for the man but for much

[5]From the material published with *Moby Dick*, ed. Harrison Hayford and Herschel Parker (New York, 1967), p. 542. After writing my argument, I was pleased to find in the most recent book on hand about Melville a central use of the same passage. See Edgar A. Dryden, *Melville's Thematics of Form; The Great Art of Telling the Truth* (Baltimore, 1968).

[6]*Pierre, Or the Ambiguities* (New York, 1957), p. 56.

in his specific fictions. But tormented unbelief, like any other ambivalence, must finally achieve, even if just by default, some sort of resolution. However scared, riddled, ambiguous, covert, uncertain, cunning, sceptical, and anguished, there is an essential meaning, if not a deer in the woods, to Melville. In one word, as "world of lies" suggests, that meaning is "nihilism."

In due course, numerous qualifications need to be made to this nihilism and, when dealing with art, the argument must always be given some finesse. Yet there may be some merit in candidly starting with a bald insistence on the primary perception. Nihilism is the only way for one who, like his own Ishmael in *Moby Dick*, "goes for a cool collected drive at death and destruction."[7] Since Melville-as-nihilist is not the main emphasis of most of the studies, and certainly not the conveniently decorous view of an "American classic," how best get such a view a hearing? How present it to the doubting, not to mention the indignant, student of Melville?

No doubt there may be several ways of attempting this. One approach might be the metapsychological analysis of the biography—something like Sartre on Baudelaire or Genêt. While less fantastic, Melville is equally peculiar, though our pedagogical familiarity tends to obscure it. Without ruling out such a critical strategy, it nonetheless appears difficult because of some inadequacy for this purpose of the biographical materials as well as some inadequacy of this critic. Melville's known life lacks directly perceivable expression of much that appears in his writings. His demonic Ahab qualities, for instance, must certainly be in the man, but they hardly show up in the biography. Though most of his adult life was spent as a professional writer and civil servant, even the few years as sailor seem not especially flamboyant or extreme. The extremity of Melville's works, probably formed around guilty fantasy, might better be focused in other ways than biographical criticism.

Part of the price of a learned way to literature—any learned

[7]*Moby Dick*, p. 197.

approach, even those self-consciously narrow and defensively analytic ones of the recent past lumped together as the "New Criticism"—must pay for the literary experience by presenting a context. Even now, the most common scholarly strategies for providing a context depend upon the dubious means of nineteenth century positivistic scholarship—"sources" and "influences." Though usually trivial in themselves—they tell us as much about art as a menu tells us about a man—these background studies do suggest some concerns and implications. For example, the sources of *Benito Cereno* in the documentary literature of the sea (an indisputable case, unlike most source studies) do not lead us, except perhaps by contrast, to the distinctive meanings of the story, but they do suggest Melville's attempt to define something characteristically American. On the broader issue of literary "relationships," some interesting things can be said of Melville's positive responses to Hawthorne and negative responses to Emerson. Yet the disparities between Melville and his American contemporaries may be even more informative. Therefore, some scholars have gone abroad. Melville's reactions to Shakespeare seem rather more suggestive than any of his American relationships.[8] Other European writers, including Carlyle (as several recent critics have argued, and perhaps over-argued), Dickens (as I shall later indicate), and Schopenhauer (at least as confirming pessimism in his *Billy Budd* period), seem relevant to Melville.[9] But far more significance can be found, as several scholars have argued, in placing Melville in the broad context of European-American romantic mythology.[10] I suggest going a step

[8]This broadness of approach, I take it, was part of the reason for the wide influence of such criticism as that of F. O. Matthiessen, *American Renaissance* (New York, 1941).

[9]The specific references for these will be cited in the following discussions of the short novels.

[10]For example, this was even done by Perry Miller, though in a paradoxical argument which turned Melville back into the romanticism which he attacked. "Melville and Transcendentalism," *Virginia Quarterly Review*, XXIX (Autumn 1953).

further and associating Melville's work with anti-mythic post-romanticism in Western culture. Quite possibly pertinent to Melville would be the broader *Zeitgeist* of Western culture in the time in which he lived. As we now recognize, there was a major developing literary-philosophical tradition which carried from Melville's time into our own: existentialism. The issue here is not at all "sources," nor even what is usually meant by "influences," but something more pervasive, less conscious, and finally a sense of direction of sensibility in response to the crumbling of the gods by which most men, but not Melville, still thought they lived.

To suggest a Melville-as-existentialist at least has the merit of countering some of the parochialism which still marks much of American literary scholarship. Perhaps the critic could make such a case by delineating parallels with Melville's writings and recognized examples of existentialism. Such efforts, however, often seem more ponderous than persuasive.[11] I propose instead the *possible* relevance of existentialism and therefore frame discussions of Melville's works with views and concerns drawn from that tradition.[12]

A critic can only hope that the concerns seem appropriate, the ideas and insights pertinent to the experience of Melville's works. I am aware that further justification for the context I employ would tend to be circular. Thus: on analytic grounds I find Melville to be similar to the existentialists in cast and centered as

[11]See one of the few ostensibly existential discussions of Melville: Maurice Friedman, *Problematic Rebel* (New York, 1963), pp. 77-98. There are, of course, passing comments in a relevant vein, such as Albert Camus identifying Melville as one on the great philosophical novelists of the "absurd." *The Myth of Sisyphus* (New York, 1955), pp. 75-76. Perhaps some of his following reflections might also help in defining the peculiar tone of Melville—"that exercise in detachment and passion. . . ."

[12]This fusion of literary criticism with other concerns is generally antithetical to what have been the dominant theories of scholarly criticism in the recent past. See, for example, Northrup Frye, *Anatomy of Criticism* (Princeton, N. J., 1957). I suggest that such approaches to the literary experience would neutralize what Melville called his "furious tropes."

they were on the problems of nihilism. I therefore take texts and issues which show some of the same concern and cast and identify them as a "tradition" which serves to explain the texts out of which I made the tradition in the first place. That is not a very satisfactory method, though probably no more specious than the usual development of critical contexts. Our widely accepted ways of speaking of, say, "the Christian tradition" or the "American literary heritage" seem equally circular. Patently, there is no Christian tradition, or—same thing—there are hundreds of them, diverse, antithetical and often quite "un-Christian." Similarly, I doubt that there is a truly identifiable American literature (or heritage, or tradition, or continuity, or whatever) though I too often lecture about it.[13] There may be dozens and hundreds of clusters of U. S. citizen-writers using the *English* language and dominantly influenced by some aspect or other of European (and only secondarily American) culture.[14] Loosely, it may make about half-sense to treat some of these clusters as belonging to an extended cultural family, if we allow it to include considerable illegitimacy. But even that analogy, in a society which disintegrated actual as well as metaphoric extended families, and in a culture often exploitative and fraudulent, may not be very persuasive. No doubt we shall have to sometimes speak, if we wish to get certain things said, as if there were American, or Christian, or existentialist, traditions. But it would be foolish to take ourselves, or anybody else, literally and to imagine that we can map

[13]However, a critic can discover how vehemently others hold to an "American literary tradition" by their outraged responses when he suggests a radical modification to it, as I did. For but two examples, see "The Prophet's Passional Ethos: Henry David Thoreau," *Punch*, 24 (December 1964), and *The Literary Rebel* (Carbondale, Ill., 1965).

[14]A major twentieth century example, never significantly explored in scholarship, would be "American surrealism," primarily the product of American writers living in France between the wars and influenced far more by French writers than any American literature. They created a heritage and continuity which has never adequately been discussed—Nathaneal West, Henry Miller, the post-World War II *avant garde*, the "black humorists" of the 1960s, etc. One of their major imperatives was to go beyond, and outside, the American literary traditions.

all the cultural swamp because we have caught some real literary frogs.

Surely one can suggestively argue that there are concerns and materials and responses which *in part* seem especially American—not least, sometimes, while seeming especially existential—and I will do so with Melville. But let us grant that, as with most literary contexts, we deal in hypotheses never adequately verifiable. The first premise in talking about things American probably should be that of a famed—and dare I say representative?—American poet: "America? It doesn't exist." The more pedestrian moral would be that America doesn't quite make sense.

My treatment of Melville, then, as an American existential nihilist provides a modest hypothesis in the effort to make some further sense of his works and such views. The admitted danger here may be like the yarn Melville recounts in *Moby Dick* of a seaman mistaking a whale for a reef; the error entered the charts and became "fact" and tradition. However, neither historical pendantry nor cultural nationalism will give us better navigational ways to keep off whales and reefs. To literally concentrate on many of the obvious characteristics of Melville—say, his autodidactic and "Victorian" sententiousness, his over-asserted masculinity (which includes mawkish patriotism, a sentimental blindness to the feminine, and a rather punitive homoeroticism), or his heavy overlay of conventional Protestant virtues—would be to over-emphasize the effluvia of American culture.

Certainly criticism should be critical, and I insist on the limitations in each work, such as the ambivalence and confusion in *Billy Budd,* the melodramatic moralism in *Benito Cereno,* and the mawkish touches in *Bartleby.* But even these might best be seen in relation to such issues as rebellion against illegitimate authority, "the Negro problem" (more properly, white racist consciousness), "the American character" (more accurately, the destructive puritan-utilitarian cast of benevolent rationalism) and certain other nihilistic responses associated with, but certainly not confined to, a continuum of American thought and feeling.

Perhaps these need no further justification than their possible presence in the literature and their pertinence to us. To emphasize them is purposive criticism—if you wish, tendentious criticism. At least the reader can know where the explication is going and what the interpretation intends to do, including going beyond the literature. Granted, Melville perplexes all such issues. We should appreciate the perplexities but then attempt to resolve them, to go beyond the perplexity. To what? Finally to that fusion of thought and feeling and choice, that passion, which wants not only to change our sense of the world but change the world itself.

CHAPTER TWO

BILLY BUDD
AND CONSERVATIVE
NIHILISM

1. *Allegorical Politics*

Some of the significance of Melville's *Billy Budd, Sailor (An Inside Narrative)*[1] might be focused with the suggestive misuse of the short novel by the noted conservative political philosopher Hannah Arendt. In her existential study of the theoretical implications for our time of the French and American revolutions, entitled *On Revolution,* she discusses Melville's fable as the major example of a poetic genius showing the "tragic and self-defeating enterprise" of Rousseauism and Jacobin revolutionism. She comments only on the political implications of the allegorical main action. There an impressed boyish sailor, Budd, is falsely accused of conspiracy to mutiny by a malicious petty officer, Claggart, in front of the British warship's commander, Vere. Unable to respond because of an emotional speech defect, Budd spasti-

[1]Ed. Harrison Hayford and Merton M. Sealts, Jr. (Chicago, 1962), pp. 43-142. Because of the many brief quotations, I do not cite individual page references to the story. References, however, are given for the notes and other apparatus of this useful edition. My one exception to this edition concerns the rejected material printed as "Preface" to earlier editions. While it may be rejectable on textual grounds, it is by Melville, it does relate to the themes of *Billy Budd,* and it has become established as an historical issue in the critical scholarship. Therefore, it is discussed in the final section of this chapter.

cally lashes out with his fist. The blow kills the petty officer. The wartime drumhead trial, called and completely controlled by Captain Vere, ends hanging Budd, though all agree he is innocent of mutiny and murder. The main push of Arendt's interpretation makes sailor Budd Rousseauean goodness, petty officer Claggart traditional evil, and commander Vere political virtue.

Melville especially . . . knew how to talk back directly to the men of the French Revolution and to their proposition that man is good in a state of nature and becomes wicked in society. This he did in *Billy Budd* . . . its topic is goodness beyond virtue and evil beyond vice. . . . Both are outside society . . . natural goodness, though it "stammers" and cannot make itself heard and understood, is stronger than wickedness. . . . It is at this point [the destruction of evil by goodness] that virtue in the person of Captain Vere is introduced into the conflict between absolute good and absolute evil, and here the tragedy begins. Virtue—which perhaps is less than goodness but still alone capable "of embodiment in lasting institutions" [quoting Vere]— must prevail at the expense of the good man as well; absolute natural innocence, because it can only act violently, is "at war with the peace of the world and the true welfare of mankind" [again quoting Vere], so that virtue finally interferes not to prevent the crime of evil but to punish the violence of absolute innocence. Claggart [Vere immediately announces] was "struck dead by an angel of God! Yet the angel must hang!" . . . "lasting institutions" break down not only under the onslaught of elemental evil but under the impact of absolute innocence as well. The law . . . cannot but punish elemental goodness even if the virtuous man, Captain Vere, recognizes that only the violence of this goodness is adequate to the depraved power of evil. The absolute . . . spells doom to everyone when it is introduced into the political realms.

Clearly, Melville reversed the primordial legendary crime. . . . It is as though he said: Let us suppose that from now on the foundation stone of our political life will be that Abel slew Cain. Don't you see that from this deed of violence the same chain of wrong-doing will follow, only that now mankind will not even have the consolation that the violence it must call crime is characteristic of evil men only?[2]

Literary objections to this consoling interpretation, a defense of the destructiveness of accepted and official "virtue," should be obvious. Arendt makes the elementary critical mistake of repeatedly using a character's words, those of Vere, as if they were not only the author's sole sincere statements but the point and purpose of the story. She ignores all possibilities of irony and ambiguity in a writer famously dedicated to them. Perhaps more crucial, this mechanical allegory of a reading quite ignores the peculiarities of the tale, such as that its many digressions and epilogues must modify the significance of the simple fable.[3] More than literary awareness is involved here. A fundamental aesthetic principle has been violated: Self-conscious art modifies and varies and qualifies the myths and allegories of mankind. That is much of the art of art, and why we must be sensitive to the telling as well as to what is told, which insistently condition each other.

Though Arendt's reading of *Billy Budd* seems dubiously done, the political issue and interpretation remain and still deserve our consideration. Nor should we dismiss her argument because of some fairly apparent contradictions, such as the concluding appeal to an absolute against founding political order in violence when she has just previously insisted that no absolutes can be "introduced into the political realm." All parties in the warship

[2]Hannah Arendt, *On Revolution* (New York, 1965), pp. 77-83. I am quoting selectively, though I hope fairly, from her arguments about *Billy Budd*. Some of the collateral issues she raises, such as her strangely eighteenth century "faculty" psychologizing of "compassion" versus "reason," are eliminated here. Because of academic compartmentalization, Arendt's discussion seems to have been ignored by Melville scholars and does not even appear in the recent bibliographies such as that of the editor in *Melville's Billy Budd and the Critics*, Second Edition, ed. William Stafford (Belmont, Calif., 1968).

[3]There is, of course, some inevitable unfairness in setting up the argument around a work of literature with a philosopher who tends to be obtuse in that area. Arendt's undiscriminating taste for large moral-political allegory is evident elsewhere, as in her praise of William Faulkner's worst novel, *A Fable*, in *The Human Condition* (New York, 1958), p. 351.

◄§ 18 §►

world of Melville's story—Budd, Claggart and Vere—depend on violence, though that of the sailor is spontaneous in origin and accidental in result. It should, I would argue, be seen as different, and less criminal, than the violence of the others. To argue otherwise, to refuse to make moral distinctions about kinds of violence, requires an absolute of non-violence, which Arendt doesn't really have. Even though many (but not Arendt) might well agree that all use and threat of killing is morally and politically contemptible, that hardly provides a basis for social organization. For given the coercion in all human relationships, non-violence can only be a relative—though usually admirable—tactic but not "the foundation stone of our political life."[4]

Elsewhere in her argument, Arendt more fully disguises her manipulation of political absolutes. Since she wishes to establish a narrowly restrictive "compact" for institutional arrangements on which to base enduring political freedom, she must claim absolutism even when being most anti-absolutistic. Otherwise competing absolutes, such as justice or freedom or compassion, might be called upon to override the political process institutionalized in the compact. The justification of revolution supposes that under appropriate circumstances such principles as justice or freedom take priority over any political process or institution. Even short of revolution, the crimes done in the name of the process or institution—the U. S. Constitution, British traditions, democratic procedures, or whatever—would no longer be readily justifiable. No form or order would be sacred; revolu-

---

[4]Arendt's tone is somewhat different in a later comment on *Billy Budd:* "under certain circumstances violence, which is to act without argument or speech and without reckoning with consequences, is the only possibility of setting the scales of justice right again (Billy Budd striking dead the man who bore false witness against him is the classic example)." "Reflections on Violence," *New York Review of Books,* XII (Feb. 27, 1969), p. 28. While spontaneous violence from moral rage is certainly of a quite different, and more acceptable, order than the rationalized and dehumanized use of violent power (such as Vere's) its necessity or desirability may still not be that of justice. Budd's injustice, of course, does not justify treating the spontaneous violence as mutiny and murder. Curiously, Arendt's later argument seems to contradict her earlier one—to her moral credit.

tion would be constantly legitimate—as I believe it should be—though not always desirable or practical.

The usual liberal as well as conservative arguments make the "political" process into a hidden absolute. Arendt holds that real politics is a unique civic mode of behavior superior in itself to answering modern "social questions," such as welfare and equality, and to all moral absolutes, such as "liberation" and "compassion."[5] To those especially concerned with political stability, freedom and charity are dangerous because incapable of being fully institutionalized. For those who make "lasting institutions" a political ultimate, the freedom of political society can, as with the American Founding Fathers, reasonably rest on the slavery of some man, or civil liberty supposedly reside in a culture of repression, or just order properly manifest itself—as in *Billy Budd*—with the hanging of the innocent.

Conceptually, the issue properly polarizes: either "good" lasting institutions or such principles as liberation and compassion become absolutes. While in practice we often muddle revolution and counter-revolution, the issue remains. Arendt's "compact," like the popular American arguments for "pragmatism" or "compromise" or "our democratic procedures," attempts to trick one's way around the issue. Some process or procedure becomes the unimpairable essence of politics. One claims that it isn't absolute by making it a vague method, supposedly without specific content, and describing it in such a way that it appears more "realistic" and "moderate" than other absolutes.[6] No doubt genteel counter-revolution is often more pleasant than the more virulent forms of reaction. But it is also more misleading since the self-congratulatory forms of domination and injustice pretend to refuse extremism and disorder while in truth maintaining immoderate misorder.

Arendt ends her discussion of *Billy Budd* with a counter-

[5]See *On Revolution*, especially chs. one and two.

[6]I forbear polemical citation but the application should be evident to much of contemporary American "liberal" political theory.

allegory in which she approaches the political absurdity of justifying the primordial social myth as the murder of *both* Cain and Abel. All politics, as Melville seemed to sense, threatens to turn into nihilism. But an argument's confusions do not mean it lacks relevance or importance. Readers more responsive to Melville's art, and more consistent political mythicizers, draw similar morals around *Billy Budd*. Many take the vicious Vere as the embodiment of moral and political virtue, as does Arendt, and eagerly sanction his murder of a boy only responsible at most for accidental manslaughter (if not deserving of reward for justifiable homicide of a false witness and *agent provocateur*).[7] Thus the larger issues of moral and political ordering needs must be discussed in relation to *Billy Budd*.

Since the posthumous publication of Melville's story in the 1920s, repeated and insistent moral-political readings have been made.[8] The "conservative" interpretations argue for the hanging of innocence, and Melville's affirmation of it, on various grounds, including moral expediency, social and historical necessity, the Hobbesian nature of order, the dangers of goodness, and the redemptive power of tragic crime. In the earlier arguments to support such views, a biographical cliché seems central: the old and dying rebel Melville converted to a submissive view of harsh authority. Thus his last prose fiction constitutes a final will and testament to this orthodoxy. As might be expected, biographical material is used but, at best, only ambiguously supports this "conversion" view. Later conservative readings, such as Arendt's, incline to an allegorical fundamentalism which makes the work's political crassness at one with artistic simplicity, if not simple-

[7]For representative examples see *Melville's Billy Budd and the Critics*, especially the articles by E. L. Grant Watson, Wendell Glick, W. Y. Tindall, Richard Harter Fogle, and Milton R. Stern.

[8]See, in the above collection, the essays by Raymond Weaver, John Middleton Murry, Lewis Mumford, Grant Watson, and William Braswell. The end-of-life repentance pattern, I suggest, merits biographical as well as artistic-intellectual doubts.

mindedness.[9] If this lengthy story only presents the obvious action of evil and innocence and just authority, then its artistic coherence must be put in doubt. Among other difficulties, why does it take so much space to make a paean to the captains of the world? Prayers to what-is need only be short.

The countering views of *Billy Budd*, developed in the 1950s and 1960s, and generally but not always "liberal" and rationalist in emphasis, usually insist on an "ironist" reading.[10] These argue for a reversed tone and dramatic technique in the story which at its fullest becomes an "inverted allegory"[11] satiric of political authority, mocking of Christian morality, and rebellious against an unjust order. However, ironist readings threaten to become an endless labyrinth. Like conspiratorial theories of history—the anti-Warren Report studies of the John Kennedy assasination furnish recent examples—the double-reading of events leads to fantastic and unresolvable involutions.[12] As with imposing a total system of magic on the universe, not lack of logic but an excessive consistency, an ornate totalism of hidden explanation, makes the world a paranoid plan. If *Billy Budd* be such an elaborately secret allegory, its role as art would be, as with other such documents, tedious and trivial to all but the exclusive few who commit themselves to that hyperlogical and fearful vision. Only

[9]For example, see Tyrus Hillway, *Herman Melville* (New York, 1963), pp. 141 ff.

[10]One of the first of these was Joseph Schiffman, "Melville's Final Stage, Irony: A Re-examination of 'Billy Budd' Criticism," *American Literature*, XXII (May 1950), pp. 128-136. A good later detailing of the ironist case, and citation of similar views, is Paul Withim, "*Billy Budd:* Testament of Resistance," *Modern Language Quarterly*, XX (July 1959), pp. 115-127.

[11]Lawrance Thompson, *Melville's Quarrel With God* (Princeton, N. J., 1952), p. 353. Thompson's sometimes suggestive discussion illustrates many of the weaknesses summarized below. Though undoubtedly right in seeing anti-authoritarianism and anti-Christianity in Melville, the attribution of a conspiratorial consistency and a mock-narrator become so forced that at times even Thompson must admit Melville's other attitudes towards his material, as on pp. 405 and 407-8. Unlike most of the ironist readings, Thompson's denies any sympathy with anti-authoritarian and anti-religious views, describing them as "adolescent."

[12]For instance, Richard Popkin's *The Second Oswald* (New York, 1967).

some commonsensical outside confirmation can make the conspiratorial or secretly ironist schemes even available to unbelievers. It would take a miracle, or an explicit confession by the criminal or author, to persuade most of us of the likelihood of a total conspiracy or ironic system since they defy much of ordinary experience and thought and action.

Melville left no instructions that would point most readers to either a literal or ironist reading of *Billy Budd*. What usable evidence we have, such as his earlier writings, seems ambiguous. We can use it—after all, it was the same mind at work—but its mixture of mystification and scepticism, irony and direct statement, will hardly be conclusive on how to view *Billy Budd*. We have one other body of evidence: the manuscript. Recent analyses of this suggest some commonsensical restrictions on interpretation. *Billy Budd* is probably not a finished work and not a fully consistent one. Perhaps because of Melville's own ambivalence, suggested by revisions over some years which markedly change the focus, characterization and tone of the story, it could not be finished or consistent.[13] Melville and his readers might appropriately respond with some incertitude and inconsistency to some of the perplexed issues of *Billy Budd*.

If *Billy Budd* is worth bothering with, *some* ironist readings, but far short of a magical-paranoid view, seem essential since much of the story does not make sense on the literal allegorical reading. But in responding to Melville as both ironic and perplexed, and his last fiction as an imperfect and mixed work, we cannot escape the questions of moral meaning and political implication. Finally, I think it must be granted, such interpretation and evaluation cannot solely arise from the materials at hand—they rest on a basis outside the story and Melville, a par-

---

[13]"The cumulative effect . . . of his . . . deletions and insertions . . . was to throw into doubt not only the rightness of Vere's decision and the soundness of his mind but also the narrator's own position. . . ." Hayford and Sealts, "Editor's Introduction," *Billy Budd*, p. 34. Their question—"is Billy Budd a unified work of art?"—should, I argue, be given a limited affirmative. Secondary inconsistencies still allow an over-all pattern and attitude.

ticular view of the political world and moral choice. Thus I have started with what I take to be the wrongheaded, if not wronghearted (for what else can you call such eagerness to justify the killing of Billy Budd?), political philosophy of Hannah Arendt. Necessarily, I must end up arguing a different politics.

The advantage of a philosopher with a text is that of taking up a problem and ignoring much of the text, which Arendt does. At least that may be preferable to the pedantry of textualism which ends up ignoring most of the problem. From the interpretations as well as the text, the largest issues of political values seem relevant to *Billy Budd*. The political philosopher is not wrong in drawing an argument around this fable, only wrong in not drawing an argument more responsive and more true, which might also be one far more conservative *and* far more radical than dreamed of in most political allegorizing.[14]

2. *The Trinity*

Of the three main figures in *Billy Budd*, the entitling character, as in *Bartleby* and *Benito Cereno*, centers the fable but does not provide the dominant consciousness and dramatic concern.[15] While Billy Budd appears to be a positive figure, and rather more so than the victims of the other short novels, he, too, focuses an odd mixture of the sympathetic and sardonic. The usual critical emphasis makes much of Melville's ornate heroization of Budd, especially the analogies with Christ and Adam. They are there but we might counter-balance the account by noting some of the qualifications which perplex the allegorical use of Christianity, finally, I believe, undercutting it.

[14]I am suggesting that the ambiguity is more thematic than textual. "Melville was never able to make up his mind" about some of the issues raised by the role of Vere, argues Kenneth Ledbetter, "The Ambiguity of *Billy Budd*," *Texas Studies in Language and Literature,* IV (Spring 1962), p. 131.

[15]Though the parallels are not usually noted, one published card file provides six groups of similarities between *Bartleby* and *Billy Budd*. H. Bruce Franklin, *The Wake of the Gods, Melville's Mythology* (Stanford, Calif., 1963), pp. 189-190.

Arendt is about half-right in treating Budd as Rousseau's Noble Savage, though the specific context, as indicated by the benign merchant ship Budd first serves on, *Rights of Man,* is Paine.[16] Most readers agree that Melville sharply qualifies romanticism by insisting on something like original sin. Thus he specifies that the beautiful, sweet, strong, good young Budd— cynosure of the Handsome Sailor—reveals an Edenic defect and fatal flaw: his stutter. Unable to speak when excited, his frustration explodes in physical violence. Allegorist Melville avoids psychological exploration of the deeper malaise symptomized by the stutter, though a possible pattern might be made of Budd as an abandoned baby and a righteously anti-sexual young man.[17] Some readers, including Arendt, insist on Billy's strength against evil, apparently because of his anti-sexuality, simple moral anger, and strong fist. But in many other ways the naive sailor appears exceptionally weak—docile, unintelligent, imperceptive, purposeless. He may, as his admiring merchant captain on the *Rights of Man* explained, reveal the peacemaker magic, "a virtue . . . sugaring the sour ones," but it melts against real evil. Melville generally makes much of the inadequacy of young and pure innocence against the malignant world.

Is it goodness, or something else, when Budd makes no "demurr" to his military enslavement when forcibly taken from the *Rights of Man* to serve as sailor on the British warship *Belli-*

[16]For a summary of the usual popular notions of the Noble Savage, see John B. Noone, Jr., *"Billy Budd:* Two Concepts of Nature," *American Literature,* XXIX (Nov. 1957), pp. 249-262.

[17]More elaborate psychoanalytic interpretation may be found in Richard Chase, *Herman Melville* (New York, 1949). Except for the father-son motif, this does not seem central. Even Chase points out that the story works mostly in abstract ways. Claggart's obsession with Budd certainly shows large nuances of homoerotic sadism but Melville explicitly insists on more than that. Yet the sexual certainly needs emphasis because of oddly bland views of Claggart-Vere. For example, see Charles A. Reich, "The Tragedy of Justice in *Billy Budd,*" *Yale Review,* LVI (Spring 1967), p. 373. He compares the Melville with Lawrence's "The Prussian Officer" and decently misses the point in both. For the pattern of homoerotic destructiveness in the latter, see my *Art of Perversity* (Seattle, Wash., 1962), Ch. I.

potent? Incapable even of a "satirical turn" of mind and tongue, he submits completely and with uncomprehending "fatalism" to his impressment, as later to all the arbitrary authority and, finally, to his unjust hanging. Without denying Billy's "goodness," we must see it not only as limited but emphatically inadequate. Why such exalted "innocence"—compared to charming Apollo, natural Hercules, otherworldly angel, prelapsarian Adam and sacrificial Christ—should occasionally explode in righteous rage seems unclear, except for the need of Melville's plot. The action essentially contradicts the poetic rhetoric. The arbitrariness of a passive-and-violent pattern of goodness can only point to Melville's ambivalence.

Other weaknesses in Billy include his epicene appeal; he properly provokes "an ambiguous smile in one or two harder faces among the blue-jackets" and what seems to be a subterranean sexual-sadistic passion in Master at Arms Claggart. Note, also, the many little derogatory touches imbedded in Melville's praising rhetoric. This "Adam before the fall" is "little more than an upright barbarian." He reveals as much "self-consciousness . . . as we may reasonably impute to a dog of Saint Bernard's breed." Elsewhere, too, he is compared, in his "dumb expressiveness" and submissiveness to his Captain, to "a dog of generous breed" but of limited "canine intelligence." Budd's understanding, "such as it was," would mark him as stupid if it were not for his charmingly indiscriminate eagerness. With an "utter innocence" hardly to be distinguished from "blank ignorance," and a "simple courage lacking experience," he is more of a puppy than a person. Billy proves repeatedly incapable of even rudimentary insight, such as the portentous warnings offered by the old sailor Dansker. Surely Billy's stutter, then, symbolizes stupidity and ineffectiveness as well as Edenic imperfection.

"Giving no cause of offense to anybody," pathologically loyal to the navy that mistreats him and the Captain who hangs him, childishly prudish and ignorant and passive and loveable, the sweet, simple sailor lacks most heroic and noble dimensions in dramatic fact, though Melville's rhetoric tries to sometimes suggest larger qualities. Budd's righteous submissiveness—not any rebellion—leads to his "crime" and death. Rather than being not of this world, Billy Budd is a pathetic case of over-conformity to it. This sweet fool is no neolithic nobleman but something less than a man, however charming. Though sweet, and certainly deserving of any decent man's defense from a predatory world, this "innocence" is not heroic, not tragic, and probably should not be considered, by Arendt and others, as moral "goodness." In fact, Melville has mocked the Noble Savage by denobling him. Billy Budd serves as a parody of "natural goodness" as well as the unjustly destroyed innocent and image of sacrificial pathos.[18]

Melville surely does talk back to advocates of simple-minded deductions about man's natural goodness, but in a more jaundiced way than usually described.[19] As we shall discuss later, no goodness can even result from Billy's suffering and destruction. What Budd does do is arouse human malignity. The obvious case Melville makes for this centers on the diabolical Master at Arms, Claggart. Presented as metaphysical evil, a "depravity according to nature," Melville argues, against sentimentalists and ameliorists, that this should not be reduced to "vicious training." Claggart is not "natural man"; no brute or primitive, he operates as something much worse, a destructive man with power "dominated by intellectuality." Of such, the narrator reflects:

[18]Such parody, of course, hardly attacks Rousseau's profound arguments for "natural" simplicity and equality and responsiveness *within* civilization, which is the main issue, nor a modern Rousseauist's awareness of the lost harmonies of neolithic culture. For scattered comments on the latter, see Claude Levi-Strauss, *Triste Tropique* (New York, 1961).

[19]Obviously I am not trying to give a full description of Budd but only important motifs which also happen to counter some fashionable interpretations. A few other commentators have also noted some negative aspects of the Handsome Sailor and that Melville "condemns not only Claggart, but Captain Vere and perhaps even Billy as well." John Bernstein, *Pacifism and Rebellion in the Writings of Herman Melville* (The Hague, Netherlands, 1964), p. 203. Though not much developed in this pleasant but unanalytic discussion, the view is certainly more serious than the uncritical apotheosis of Budd, as in R. W. B. Lewis, *The American Adam* (Chicago, 1955), pp. 146 ff.

"Toward the accomplishment of an aim which in wantonness of malignity would seem to partake of the insane, he will direct a cool judgment sagacious and sound." He thus elaborates plans to entrap Billy, whose innocence and beauty offend him, in the appearance of mutiny because he shrewdly judges that rigid Captain Vere will fully do his evil work for him. Correctly reasoned, as the later action demonstrates, though he did not forsee the stuttering rage which would produce the blow which improbably cost him his life. Claggart, however, did achieve the destruction of Billy Budd.

"An uncommon prudence is habitual with the subtler depravity," comments Melville in a perceptive cut at the orthodox moralist's exaltation of prudence. Intellectual, prudent, systematic, Claggart represents the social and moral order in his role as chief naval policeman aboard the frigate. Such men, says Melville, do not just result from ignorance, social disorder or self-interest (either "mercenary" or "sensual"), but from civilization as a whole. Here Melville mocks, yet again, ideas of optimistic amelioration as well as ego psychology. For Claggart embodies the moral order in his ingratiating "deference" to authority, in his decorous "respectability," and in his stern "patriotism," as well as in his rationalized malignancy. Depravity wears conventional values comfortably and well—with good cause.

Portrayed also as a darkly pallid and mysteriously degenerated aristocrat, Claggart derives, in a literary way, from the romantic Satan—a rationalistic and civilized figure of deracination as with Ivan Karamazov's devil—and from the Gothic novel's personification of the horrific as the decayed and wicked aristocrat. Claggart can also be related to the historically developing pattern of the diabolical criminal-cop and secret agent. If the characterization of Budd mocks the goodness of natural innocence, orthodox moralists cannot take much solace from the prudently rational superiority of Claggart who epitomizes civilized official evil. Radical libertarian theories, of course, need not deny such evil—

here twentieth century radicals often contrast with those of the Enlightenment—because bad institutions can be seen as compounding, rather than just creating, malignancy. Claggarts in power provide an obvious case for revolt. But, to give conservatives their due, where Jacobins can go badly wrong is not in overthrowing the power of the Claggarts but in assuming to create similar power without compounding similar evil.

Melville's "innocence" (not "goodness") and "malignity" seem Pyrrhic in the usual moral terms. Budd as a stupid natural-Christ versus Claggart as a prudently rational Satan provides a canted rather than orthodox allegory. The sardonic mythicizing, including with Claggart the motif of the trickster tricked, could be more fully elaborated. But my interpretation, though more harsh than most, has not yet reached the crux of the disagreements about *Billy Budd*. I need not dispute further with those who want to summarize this part of the allegory as innocence-evil, Christ-Satan, so long as they allow for considerable and peculiar slanting in Melville's treatment of them.[20] Nor would I dispute with those many interpreters of Melville who then want to move on and complete the Christian metaphor of the trinity—the evidence is clear that such images preoccupied Christian-anti-Christian Melville—so long as they recognize the rest of the ambiguity and parody. We may thus accept the magisterial and virtuous appearing Vere as the father-God of the allegory, but one in which he functions as an authoritarian whose divinity reveals the larger form of the rationally prudent madness of his plotting servitor, Claggart. Vere's command and benevolence end horrendously destructive—the true father deity as vicious virtue.

As I read history, the great crimes—the imperial conquests, the inquisitions, the religious wars, the genocidal persecutions, the Nazi and Stalinist totalitarianisms, the Western saturation-

---

[20]Similar doubts about the centrality of the dominant allegorical interpretations are made, but in a very narrow context and unimportant interpretation, by Warner Berthoff, *The Example of Melville* (Princeton, N. J., 1962), pp. 186 ff.

and-atomic bombings—did not claim wicked motives or the desire for malignacy but rationality, prudence, interest, and virtue. The direct pursuit of evil, of depravity, of despoliation, of hatred and destruction, seem self-limiting motives. How much bad can a man do? A great deal only if he claims, to himself and to others, to be doing the good. Like Vere. The Captain carries further Claggart's "judgment sagacious and sound" serving "malignancy," and a "prudence" suitable and habitual to "the subtler depravity." As presented, Captain Vere thoroughly believes in traditional virtue—patriotism, military duty, absolute authority, the repressive order, the civilization of hereditary wrongs, and the righteous war against all revolution. Though he considers Billy Budd not only innocent of mutiny and homicide but an embodiment of angelic goodness, he systematically works to destroy him in the name of those virtues.

Melville's description of the malignant intellectual—the "most dangerous sort" of madman because appearing sane and rational—applies to Vere's love-hate of Billy as well as to Claggart's, though Vere may seem the more mad because of his exalted claims to goodness. Evil as goodness quite outdoes mere evil as nastiness. The skeptical, though not very profound, ship's Surgeon suspects Vere's sanity to be "unhinged" in the Budd case. He "professionally and privately surmised" that Vere was the victim of "aberration." The narrator dryly comments that the truth of this the reader must "determine for himself." When Melville uses this manner in other works to pose an issue, it stands affirmed, as it apparently must be here.[21] The only substantial objection to the Vere-unhinged diagnosis rests on the

[21]Melville posed the major problem of Captain Delano's excessive optimism in *Benito Cereno* in a similar way. The repeated form as well as the specific evidence insist on Vere's aberration. Even Paul Brodtkorb, Jr., skittishly agrees: "If Vere is insane, he is so only insofar as society's endless circularity is. . . ." "The Definitive *Billy Budd;* But Aren't It All Sham?" PMLA, LXXXII (December 1967), p. 610. Apparently this means that Vere is mad if the society is mad—more correctly the official organization and ruling class. That would do, but in addition we must note, as the Surgeon does, Vere's obsessional and, I would add, pathological, self-mythicizing increment of personal madness.

radical implications: If Vere be mad, much that passes for ration-ality and decency and order must also be mad. To accept the diagnosis requires the threatening awareness that traditional authority is largely synonymous with aberration.

Melville's portrayal of Vere, like that of Billy Budd, contains much that undercuts the heroic proportions that some of the rhetoric suggests. We cannot ignore the prefacing digression about Admiral Nelson, for whom Melville seems to have an excessive admiration. The high praise of Nelson for his "bra-vado," for his lack of "personal prudence," for his ability to "win" over rather than "terrorize" a discontented crew, and for his brilliant style, establishes standards of heroic exaltation. As several critics have noted,[22] Vere shows up as inadequate on each of these standards of heroism of his own time, and therefore stands mocked on his own British quarter deck.

Note, too, the curious qualifications that mark even the praise of Vere. The Captain seems a "sailor of distinction," which says much for an aristocrat who, Melville reports with historical appropriateness, must have gotten his advancement through his connections with the "higher nobility." In action, prudent Vere showed himself "intrepid . . . though never injudiciously so"—a mocking twist, and quite alien to the standard set by Nelson. Vere is "mindful of the welfare of his men, but never tolerating an infraction of discipline"—a gross contradiction, easily con-firmed by military history as well as military experience. Given the naval order, especially then, it would be quite impossible to maintain the welfare of the sailors and be a strict disciplinarian. Generally, too, in those mutinous times as well as in others, the literalist commanders were the least successful. The suggestions that Vere might be viewed as a "martinet" and compared to a Byzantine tyrant fit the same pattern, as do the dramatic specifics

[22]Several of my points are indebted to the articles previously cited (note 10, above) by Schiffman and Withim. See also Joan Joffe Hall, "The Historical Chap-ters in *Billy Budd*," *University Review*, XXX (Oct. 1963), pp. 35-40.

of Vere's behavior. No contrasting characteristics show this Captain as unusually heroic or otherwise distinguished. Melville quite savages the figure he apparently praises in such remarks as "whatever his sturdy qualities he was without brilliant ones."

When we come to the description of Vere as a man of character with "a marked leaning toward everything intellectual," we should be prepared, as readers of Melville's other works, for a mocking edge. A recurrent pattern in Melville's stories criticizes figures of "higher truth" (suggested here in the very name Starry Vere) and intellectualism as against more intuitive senses of awareness. The Captain's intellectualism, clearly identified as "pedantic," leads him to books only to confirm his "settled convictions." The narrator points out that Vere goes beyond the other reactionary members of the privileged class, who feared the revolution because of the threat to their privileges, to abhor its ideas on principle because "incapable of embodiment in lasting institutions . . . for the true welfare of mankind." This quasi-Burkeanism (repeatedly cited by Arendt) provides standard class ideology. Yet Melville also insists on seeing Vere as "exceptional" in his moral seriousness and dutiful competence, above the usual naval officer of his time. Though hardly high praise, we probably should see Vere as the best that such a social and political order will normally place in authority. Nelsons, of course, were rare. To the degree that we can see Vere as a consistent representative of authority, he seems a well-intentioned and would-be moral man superior to the many foul commanders and his social class in a vicious system.

The impressment of seamen, the miserable conditions of sailor life, the cruel and arbitrary discipline, the sadistic flogging, the use of malicious police spies (and the assignment of Claggart),[23] and an utterly outrageous system of military justice, go beyond Captain Vere's choice, though he unquestioningly accepts them. To use a more recent but still appropriate analogy, the best com-

[23]In one of the better books on Melville, Merlin Bowen emphasizes the unity of Vere and Claggart. *The Long Encounter, Self and Experience in the Writings of Herman Melville* (Chicago, 1960), pp. 218 ff.

mandant of a concentration camp does not have much of a moral argument going for him. But Vere's nasty authoritarianism also shows certain individual dimensions, elliptically presented by Melville. Violating usage, sense, and his own suspicions of the unsavory Claggart, Vere sets up a personal confrontation between Claggart and Budd. First ordering Billy to answer the malicious mutiny charge, then encouraging him to take his time, he establishes a violent tension in the outraged but submissive boy who wants to prove himself to his paternalistic commander. Vere thus provides the immediate cause for Budd's spastic and fatal lashing out at Claggart, though he shows no signs of recognizing his culpability. Here, as later, Vere switches confusingly between treating Billy as a "father" and as a "military disciplinarian," a classic perversion which usually leads to disastrous results. As Melville presents this, a larger pattern, a moral myth, reveals itself. At Claggart's death, Vere, without even further inquiry into a murky situation, magisterially pronounces his own Master at Arms to be the revealed Biblical liar: "It is the divine judgment on Ananias!" And though he has not called a military trial of Budd, not even an investigation of a sailor he knew very little about, he immediately announces a mad moral judgment and a totally antithetical sentence: "Struck dead by an angel of God! Yet the angel must hang!"

What a weird Christian moralist! Is this any way to run a ship and steer a sane course towards practical human justice? Self-mythification, rather than moral justice or even naval expediency, arises from Captain Vere's responses. He apparently sees himself playing a tragic role in a bookish-divine drama—the sorrowing but vengeant father-god. All his practical behavior seems warped by the same aberrant sense of his role. In ordering strict secrecy, contrary to naval law and custom,[24] he justifies it by reference to a possible mutiny which he just previously denied

[24]For Vere's many violations of naval law and procedure, see Hayford and Sealts, "Notes and Commentary," *Billy Budd*, pp. 175 ff., and C. B. Ives, "*Billy Budd* and the Articles of War," *American Literature*, XXXIV (March 1962), pp. 31-39. They note some confusions on Melville's part but Vere's violations go beyond them.

existed and for which there is not the least evidence but the unsupported claim of a dead police spy whom Vere considers a liar. With a curiously self-dramatizing fervour, Vere hurriedly substitutes a personal drum-head trial in place of the legally required later trial on his superior's ship. His puzzled officers take this as both a violation of sea usage and common-sense, but they do not recognize Vere's urge to destructive power and self-mythicizing drama.

A further dimension of Vere's mania, which seems as obsessive as Ahab's but quieter, appears in the strangely attenuated but fervent chapter following that on the trial. Here Vere again violates naval law and custom by privately communicating the sentence of death to the condemned sailor. The narrating author takes an odd pose of reticence, contrary to other scenes, and does not give the conversation of Vere and Budd, though I find no dramatic justification for not doing so. The narrator grandiloquently "conjectures" about the meeting of Budd and Vere, "each radically sharing in the rarer qualities of our nature—so rare indeed as to be all but incredible to average minds however much cultivated. . . ." If not mockery, this incredible statement judges the characters, and rather unreasonably, while denying the reader any dramatic test for the judgment, and then assures the reader that he could not understand anyway. Such peculiarities as this in *Billy Budd* provide the basis for both theories of involuted irony in the attitude and inconsistency in the art.

The narrating author also conjectures an undescribed scene of exalted tenderness between the Captain and the condemned sailor, concluding:

The austere devotee of military duty, letting himself melt back into what remains primeval in our formalized humanity, may in the end have caught Billy to his heart, even as Abraham may have caught young Isaac on the brink of resolutely offering him up in obedience to exacting behest. But there is no telling the sacrament . . . [when] two of great nature's nobler order embrace.

Vere, then, simultaneously plays Abraham to Billy's Isaac and the death-demanding God in a world without any other redeemer to stay the primal crime. Certainly such a passage can reasonably be read as irony. Did Melville intend this? It makes little difference. For even Melville's Christian contemporary, Soren Kierkegaard, had to take the milder Abraham-Isaac-God myth as a violation of all ordinary reason, the ultimate irony of faith.[25] We must thus see the Vere-Budd, the father-son, embrace and killing, a far more extreme relation, as savagely ironical in effect.

If one insists on also finding literal elements in the scene, the positive treatment of the father embracing the son-figure he unnecessarily insists on killing should provide the main support for those wishing to argue that the dying Melville testifies in *Billy Budd* to the affirmation of vicious social and moral values. Billy's "God Bless Captain Vere" just before his hanging—a standard formality for the condemned made nauseously sincere (we should not suspect ignorant and slow-witted Billy of intentional irony)—then serves as symptom of Melville's final degradation. Some biographical confirmation might be developed in the author outliving both of his sons—the eldest a suicide at eighteen—before writing *Billy Budd*.[26] The final sentence of this chapter of the story could be used as further extension of Melville's guilty abasement in psychic son-killing; murderous fatherly Vere appears in "agony" and "the condemned one suffered less than he who had mainly effected the condemnation...." So the guilty parent might say in self-justification (the it-hurts-me-but-I-do-it-for-your-good trick we fathers practice). Official murder as an act of love carries out the most extreme Oedipal warping, love as punishment, a pathology of traditional authori-

[25]See *Fear and Trembling* (London, 1946), pp. 69 ff.

[26]The "father-god" problem may be found almost everywhere in Melville's writings, and it is partly traceable to a sense of betrayal by the failure of a father who also orphaned him. As Charles Olson gnomically summarizes the theme, Melville "agonized over paternity," "demanded to know the father," and "wanted a god." *Call Me Ishmael* (New York, 1947), p. 82.

tarianism which could be reasonably applied to Melville's biography, a father "abandoned" son who may have failed his own son. Melville as well as his character Vere might have been in a bad way in guilty madness.

Here I only mean to suggest how Melville could be identified with Vere, and the undeniable ambiguities of *Billy Budd* could be related to the deepest personal guilt and rationalization of the author. But let us return, less speculatively, to the long preceding chapter of the trial. This starts with questions about where to draw the line between "sanity and insanity" and ends with the condemnation to death of innocent Billy Budd. It seems unlikely that this would be an accidental shape to the main section of a narrative reworked over some years. Mania appears evident at the start of the trial in Vere's usurping all roles (prosecutor, witness, defense counsel, and judge) because he fears that even his best officers "might not prove altogether reliable in a moral dilemma involving aught of the tragic." The Captain, we see, desperately wants to make a tragic drama out of a pathetic accident. Hence the dramatization by way of the mock-trial when he has already announced the hanging of Billy Budd.

Captain Vere's unquestioning and untragic self-justification in the trial appear patent. When the earnest and reasonable officer of marines asks why the Master at Arms so improbably charged Budd with mutiny, Vere interposes, though he cannot plausibly know the answer, to dismiss the question as "hardly material." He adds that "a martial court must needs in the present case confine its attention to the blow's consequence." In fact, this requires no discussion since all parties, including the accused, agree that Budd struck Claggart and he died. Legally, the would-be stickler Captain argues falsely. Even the most extreme martial law—as one can find in the reports of the Nore and Spithead mutinies—must take some account of different kinds and causes of homicide, which Vere arrogantly denies. The pretended trial, then, just serves as a ritual for confirming Vere's prior sentence and sanctifying his desire to murder Billy Budd.

When Vere's officer asks for further evidence about the causes of the crime, Vere dismisses the request by shifting to his private theology: "to use a Scriptural phrase, it is 'a mystery of iniquity,' a matter for psychological theologians to discuss." The switching of a commonsense question about the inciting actions of Claggart to a metaphysical puzzle of Pauline dimensions must be seen as a trick, as is Vere's absolute separation of human and divine, naval and moral, justice. Characteristic of mainstream Christianity, principles of humility and mystery have been tortured into arrogance and authoritarianism.

The Captain then orders the questioning stopped, and Billy to silence, and proceeds to arrange the judgment and sentencing. In both substance and drama, the issue here must be the peculiarity of Vere's arguments and behavior. If we find no conflict in the appearance and reality of what Vere does, no disparity between his claims and revealed motives, then this main section of the story will lack justification. Novelistically, the trial scene would be mere verbiage if it did not in some way expose Vere and his views, for no other drama is allowed. The critic must make his choice—conflict in Vere's role or failure of art—and draw the implications for the rest of the story.

Playing god in the moral as well as the legal realm, Captain Vere announces to the officers that their uncertainty consists of a conflict "of military duty with moral scruples." These he weirdly holds to be antithetical. "How can we adjudge to summary and shameful death a fellow-creature innocent before God, and whom we feel to be so?" There would seem to be only one possible answer here, yet Vere promptly comes up with the opposite one. "It is Nature. But do these buttons that we wear attest that our allegiance is to Nature? No, to the King." He insists on the very arbitrariness of the King's law but demands that "however pitilessly that law may operate in any instance, we nevertheless adhere to it and administer it." As some readers note, there can be no mercy in this ostensible Christian who reduces justice to buttons. More formally, when monarchical rule and "natural law" can no longer be related, at least one of them must go. Though apparently not intending it, Vere suggests an overwhelming argument for the abolition of the King's law, and kings. In effect, he posits the very Jacobinism he despises. Put another way, Vere explicitly acknowledges such standards as Nature, God, civilized forms, and the moral scruples of reasonable men. Yet he nonetheless violates all of them.[27] We usually characterize such contradictoriness as madness or criminality. But it is also selfish. For when this fictional war criminal argues that martial law stands totally against morality, basing it on the analogy of war (by definition the breakdown of law and justice) rather than martial law being a special form of civil and moral law, he asserts the right of capricious force, which happens to be his.

The officer of Marines reasonably objects to Vere's arguments that "Budd proposed neither mutiny nor homicide." Instead of dismissing the man with snobbery, as he did earlier, Vere slyly agrees but concludes, "At the last Assizes it shall acquit." This carries the separation of practical and moral values into the fantastic. Confining justice solely to heaven (whether it be extra-terrestrial or, as more often these days, a futuristic society) provides the most horrendous historical rationalization of injustice, cruelty, and destruction. Plain hatred leading to murder would seem rather more decent. The man who displaces all justice in the way Vere does must be totally cynical or mad, and can hardly avoid being vicious.[28]

Nor does Vere allow mercy. When one of his officers proposes conviction but mitigation of the death penalty, Vere switches his argument to expediency. He appeals to the officers' fear of the

[27]On further reflection, Hannah Arendt should see the similarity of her political hero, Vere, and her villain of *Eichmann in Jerusalem,* especially in their moral mediocrity and banal acceptance of what is.

[28]And yet we find such moral judgments as this: "In 'Billy Budd' . . . the ideal is embodied in Captain Vere . . . [and] at the Day of Judgment Billy Budd will be vindicated." Richard Harter Fogle, *Melville's Shorter Tales* (Norman, Okla., 1960), p. 143.

Mutiny of the Nore. Acknowledging that such mutinies result from "arbitrary discipline," he nonetheless insists that lack of arbitrary discipline would bring mutiny on his ship. He also suggests that mercy would embarrass the officers—the view of the sailors is utterly contemptuous here—which even reduces the expediency to vanity. Melville must be read satirically in this section, or he is unreadable. Vere's final appeal to the brainwashed nature of the victim seems equally outrageous; he feels, he says, for Billy Budd, but believes that the condemned man's "generous nature" would sympathize with their killing him.

I find it nearly incomprehensible how some readers take Vere's justifications for killing—the brainwashed victim, the officers' vanity, the immorality of law and allegiance, the innocent victim's heavenly reward, and the legitimacy of capricious force as long as it is his own—as in any way valid. That the officers accept this mad rhetoric can partly be explained by the power and the fear that Vere plays upon, though none of them merit any admiration. Perhaps some readers get confused by Melville's emphasis on the appearances of decency and seriousness in Captain Vere. That, of course, provides devastating irony, not justification. Nor can we justify Vere by merely hypothetical mutiny—a hypothesis which the submissiveness of the crew at the hanging further proves irrelevant. The only warrant for Vere must be some reactionary ideology of maintaining, without regard to cost, the authority of the Captain as the expression of custom, law, form, or, as Arendt avers, the need of "lasting institutions." But from the moment of the Claggart-Budd confrontation, Melville shows Vere violating usage, twisting the law, and emptying the forms. So about all we could say in Vere's defense is that he properly embodies the arbitrary and vicious institution of the warship, and in that sense may act appropriately even if illegally and unnecessarily and immorally.

However much we see the Captain as the product of a vicious system, Melville does not leave the issue there and gives Captain Vere several personal aberrations as the expression of his individual will. The man displays in all his pronouncements about Billy Budd an arrogant and ruthless sense of his sole rightness. The religious metaphors with which Melville presents him as well as some of his arguments locate part of this certitude in a mythic mania, a trinitarian tragedy in which irrevocable and unexplainable evil forces authority to destroy innocence in this world. That diabolical version of Christianity makes Vere's perversity much greater than Claggart's because it is rationalized as positive meaning, as justice and love.

Arbitrary authority, like unexplainable suffering, frequently costumes itself in religious rhetoric. So does Vere. Since Melville's tone gives way to sarcasm several times in presenting such Christianity, that, too, suggests the general ironic perspective on Vere as Christian-speaking authority. Note, for example, that ex-Calvinist Melville describes the Captain's pronouncement of Billy's death sentence to the crew as the "congregation of believers in hell listening to the clergyman's announcement of his Calvinistic text." The scene with the Christian minister carries this further. The naval chaplain visiting the condemned sailor finds that he "had no consolation to proffer which could result in a peace transcending that which he beheld." The author suggests that it is a "better thing" to die an innocent barbarian, a Noble Savage, than a Christian. Melville also sees a larger irrelevance to Christianity:

Bluntly put, a chaplain is the minister of the Prince of Peace in the host of the God of War. . . . Why, then, is he there? Because he indirectly subserves the purpose attested by the cannon; because he too lends the sanction of the religion of the meek to that which practically is the abrogation of everything but brute force.

There we have a clear statement of what Vere, defender of the lasting institutions of a Christian realm, is most fully doing: subordinating all to brute force.

Melville's tone in the hanging scene does not seem ironic. Yet it finally must be seen as serving Pyrrhic ends. A mythic moment: with the sky "a soft glory as of the fleece of the Lamb of God seen in mystical vision. . . . Billy ascended; and ascending, took the full rose of the dawn." This may be understood as a profound parody of the religious mythos. Profound because of the primordial drama of the innocent "son" destroyed in rationalized murder by the "father"; parody because dumbly submissive barbarian Billy arbitrarily crucified by the second-rate mad Captain ascends only the yardarm and brings no glad tidings and messianic hope to mankind.[29] Mythic treatment of such drama, as Melville gives it, appears equally essential and irrelevant.

Disciplinarian Vere, who used the specious threat of mutiny in browbeating his fellow officers into hanging Billy, continues to fear his crew after the hanging. Though they show no signs of rebelliousness, he punitively puts them through their paces, violating the rule against Sunday exercises.

That such variance from usage was authorized by an officer like Captain Vere, a martinet as some deemed him, was evidence of the necessity for unusual action in what he deemed to be temporarily the mood of his men. "With mankind," he would say, "forms, measured forms, are everything; and that is the import couched in the story of Orpheus with his lyre spellbinding the wild denizens of the wood." And this he once applied to the disruption of forms going on across the Channel and the consequences thereof.

Vere, of course, is violating the forms, the Sunday customs, in supposedly defending them. Furthermore, to defend the sweet Orphean music of civilization by equating it with a hanging and harsh discipline is ludicrous. It takes a reactionary mania to

[29]Contrast James E. Miller, Jr., and the view that "Billy ascends to Heaven, there to sit at the throne of God." *A Reader's Guide to Herman Melville* (New York, 1962), p. 228. This statement appears to be made in all seriousness.

pretend that such actions civilize.[30] Vere can reduce the great revolution to a mere "disruption of forms"—as if it didn't create all too many forms of its own—only by that mad egotism of the conservative that no matter what he does he maintains the verities of ordered life. All of this would be utterly silly if it were not characteristic of a certain reactionary cast of mind now as well as then.

The musical reference in this passage is carried further with the crew doing their arbitrary drills "toned by music and religious rites subserving the discipline of war." When such forms serve such false purposes they become not everything, as Vere holds, but nothing because they have lost all authenticity. We are back to allegiance to buttons; Vere demonstrates destruction masked as conservation with naval usage, Christianity, justice, and the Orphean music of joy. We need not, of course, doubt Vere's horrible sincerity, or Melville's sad mockery.

In a sequel summarizing the death of Vere, we learn that he received a fatal wound from the revolutionary ship *Athée*. Since the historical role of revolutionary atheism was to kill false gods, that seems appropriate. But (as Arendt rightly sensed) Melville sees revolutionary myths as inadequate, and the *Athée* is captured by the indomitably conservative *Bellipotent*. Here Melville seems the disinterested manipulator of allegorical comment, almost to the point of cynicism. So, too, with the final comments on Vere. The narrator suggests that in spite of his "philosophical austerity" the Captain may have carried "the most secret of all passions, ambition." Did he, then, hang Billy Budd to advance some fantasy of power, and to exalt, like the Miltonic version of the Christian deity which Melville may draw on, his own authority?

[30]How comic of Vere to identify with Orpheus! This fits the misanthropic tone of Melville's *Confidence Man*. Melville's irony may well be conscious, on the principle he noted in *Moby Dick* that allows for "that sort of superstition, which in some organizations seems to spring, somehow, from intelligence than from ignorance." Hayford and Parker (New York, 1967), p. 103.

The details certainly suggest such an extreme authoritarianism. It remains blind to the end. That Vere murmurs at his death "Billy Budd, Billy Budd," reportedly without the "accents of remorse," suggests with savage irony that he dies feeling righteous. To the end he exalts in having treated Billy as a son by murdering him, fully enclosed in a self-myth to a virtuously vicious fullness. The trinity has been destroyed, leaving us not only with an insight into why it is so horrendously difficult to change such a moral order but with a sense of the largest human pathos and fatalism.

3. Annihilating the Allegory

Billy Budd stands as a curiously undramatic work. We expect further conflict, after the initial allegorical action of innocence and malignity, Budd and Claggart, unfolds. Whether from a Miltonic design or an ambivalent incompletion, the action carries very little development. Captain Vere does not change and little conflict appears within him. The three main characters die, but not one appears remorseful, defiant, or in any other way transformed. In spite of its "adventure" scene and melodramatic deaths, *Billy Budd* remains a static story, essentially meditative rather than dramatic.

To most fully perceive what Melville means, then, we must put our emphasis on the patterns and peculiarities of the meditations. Note, for instance, that any dramatist redoing *Billy Budd* puts it in much shorter form.[31] But in Melville's treatment, digressive reflection takes over and becomes the form. Here we must discover much of the "intention" of the story. From the opening typology on "Handsome Sailors" through announced diversions on mutinies, Nelson, the class qualities of seamen, and

[31]See, for example, the dramatic adaptions of Louis O. Coxe and Robert Chapman, *Billy Budd* (Princeton, N. J., 1951), and E. M. Forester, Eric Crozier and Benjamin Britten, *Billy Budd: Opera in Four Acts* (London, 1951). My earlier references to Milton, often discussed for influence on Melville, presuppose the interpretation developed in Kingsley Widmer, "The Iconography of Renunciation," *Milton's Epic Poetry*, ed. C. A. Patrides (London, 1967).

the nature of evil, the narrative winds around the only lightly developed allegory until it ends in an ornate series of half a dozen sequels. The often portentous style also contributes to its being a small *Moby Dick* in its endless circling and progression by diversion and analogy. The effect is indirection, and its consequent feelings of ambiguity and skepticism. The author self-consciously comments in *Billy Budd* on the lack of "symmetry of form": "Truth uncompromisingly told will always have its ragged edges. . . ." The effects of the digressions and analogies and epilogues repeatedly serve to compromise the allegory in the narrative. Such contrary and incompatible or uncertain truths, then, may well be *the* truth Melville uncompromisingly pursues.

A similar point may be suggested for the variations in style. *Billy Budd* lacks the dominant single tone of many of Melville's other works and shifts from allegorical grandiloquence to harsh sarcasm. Certainly it often shows the author at his less felicitous prose, with a paucity of dramatic dialogue, a heaviness of historical and literary allusions (as with the somewhat confusing if not contradictory comparisons and metaphors for Billy Budd), and a generally sententious cast. These may also serve as ways of raising doubts about the otherwise simple action and thus provide some of the undercutting and ambiguous truth. Placing the action nearly a century back from the time of writing, to 1797, and constantly reminding the reader of yet other uncertainties due to disparate times and conditions, heightens our sense of qualification. The explanations of antique "sea usage" appear rather pedantic, though less so when we note their major function: they help to ironically point up that those who ostensibly most support tradition and custom, such as Captain Vere, most thoroughly violate them. In sum, such irregularities, such "ragged edges," in form and style and material compromise any simple moral or mythic view of the events and characters. A rough piece of goods shows through. To contend otherwise means to edit or rewrite *Billy Budd*.

The first epilogue after the hanging scene drastically qualifies the mythic tones of that scene. The Purser, a stupid man, and the Surgeon, a limited one, discuss the absence of "mechanical spasm" (and perhaps the absence of traditional ejaculation) in Billy's body at his death. Quite a shift of feeling! The Purser asks if the lack of spasm can be explained by "will-power." The Surgeon mocks the question but declines to give any alternative answer. The Purser asks if Billy beat the rope by some sort of merciful suicide. The Surgeon also refuses this answer as unscientific. Consistent with other skeptical remarks of Melville's about science, he seems to be showing here that science cannot provide the meaning; science is less truth than the thinnest of myths, the refusal of adequate human explanation.

The world necessarily creates a series of myths to explain this drama of malignity and innocence and authority. The official public one seems the most gross. In a brief chapter of sarcasm Melville presents the "authorized" naval chronicle view of the Budd case. This weekly news publication displays as much accuracy as the notorious news weeklies of our time. It confuses the origins of the characters and melodramatically fantasizes the action. Its drastically erroneous account includes high praise for the patriotism of Claggart, which is seen as moral disproof of the adage that "patriotism is the last refuge of a scoundrel." Since Melville earlier emphasized the patriotism of Claggart—and Vere—and since the news report gets harshly exposed as erroneous and bigoted, that seems to confirm the adage about patriotism. Official public myth is mostly lie.

Several other myths appear in the concluding chapter in the attempt of yet others to give shape and meaning to this forlorn episode. One of these rounds off the opening description of Billy Budd as the seaman's cynosure. (*This* symmetry suggests that Melville was talking about something deeper when he pointed to the lack of "symmetry of form.") The story of Billy Budd, we are told, carries for "some few years" beyond his death. In the sailors keeping track of the spar from which he was hung and venerating it—"To them a chip of it was as a piece of the Cross"—Melville seems to dryly suggest how popular religious myth, such as Christology, takes form, though only to fade away.[32] The quasi-crucifixion of the simple sailor also takes more directly literary form, ostensibly a sailor's ballad, "Billy in the Darbies." Unfortunately not a very interesting poem, and not a suitable image of a folk hero, this monologue-lament describes a fettered Billy awaiting death with a self-pathos and punning which falsify the simple primitive and innocent of the narrative. The fancy imagery—"A jewel-block they'll make of me tomorrow, Pendant pearl from the yard arm end"—provides a rococo irrelevance, insisting on the mere dream stuff of pathos. Poetry provides, then, just another inadequate and false apotheosis.

The sailors, the narrator says before the moony fade-out provided by the verse, felt that "the penalty was somehow unavoidably inflicted from the naval point of view, for all that they instinctively felt that Billy was a sort of man incapable of mutiny as of wilful murder." While we should not, of course, confuse the "naval point of view" with justice or any other value, the statement seems a suitable, though understated, moral for the story. The punishment of the innocent is a proper culmination of "lasting institutions."

I cannot see that Melville suggests any alternative to his mockery of mythicizing. The Christ-like treatment of the innocent barbarian was only local and temporary, as one would expect from its inappropriateness. The mythic attempts at explanation or justification by Captain Vere, by the under-officers, by the official news journal, by the sailors, and by the poet, show themselves as inadequate and inappropriate. Myths, whether as private mania, public convention, religious glorification, official lies, or poetic comment, certainly do not provide any lasting truth. Perhaps the mythic anti-myth, *Billy Budd* itself, provides

[32]This point, of course, contrasts with the many positive Adam-Christ allegorical emphases, such as those of Milton R. Stern, *The Fine Hammered Steel of Herman Melville* (Urbana, Ill., 1957), pp. 206-239.

the most enduring answer by this very destructiveness. The author's anguished skepticism would seem more confirmed than denied by the desperate efforts of many of his readers to remythicize his fable in spite of its annihilating form and logic.

Melville's multiple sequels of cancelling interpretations serve to confirm his pessimism. The form of the fable provides a Pyrrhic mockery of every usual effort to mythicize and justify the cruel and arbitrary order of "lasting institutions." The prudent malignancy, the inadequate innocence, and the vicious virtue end in fatalism and pathos.[33] The very perplexities of the uncertain narrative, of the mixed tones and ambiguities of suggestion, further this sense as the cohering "intention" of the story. Putting proper emphasis on the perplexities should not defeat responses to *Billy Budd;* instead, it should mandate stoic resistance to the ways of falsifying an unjust world and a negative universe. Though some of our fellow readers persist in taking the madly self-aggrandizing myths of the Captain Veres for the truth, or imposing their own myths on Melville, still, his awkward and melancholy and perplexed wisdom does leave one with an empowering sense of refusing to have evil benevolently rationalized into virtue.

4. *Beyond Politics?*

Does Melville's myth mocking myths deny all authority and legitimacy, and thus all politics? Both "conservative" and "liberal" readers try to qualify *Billy Budd* back into political pertinence. Arendt, as we have seen, takes a conventionally narrow view of politics and rules "evil" and "innocence" (rather dubi-

[33]An essential aspect of the tone, though not of the larger implications, is summarized by Brodtkorb as a "twilight ground where few human actions are rationally chooseable" and part of Melville's despairing effort to accept "nothingness." "The Definitive *Billy Budd*," pp. 610 and 612. In order to get a positive note not in the story, the Peter Ustinov cinematic adaption, *Billy Budd* (England, 1962), ends with the hanging but overlays it with a portentous narrating voice which announces, contrary to all probabilities, that the event contributed to the progress of justice.

ously labeled "goodness") out of the dialectic of humane order. Though she puts Budd and Claggart "outside society," which means that she sanctions their deaths, she wishes to retain Captain Vere, under the rubric of a "virtue" which is, somehow, neither good nor evil, but the special logic of political life, the support of "lasting institutions." As I have argued, the institutional authority of Vere, no matter how rationalized as virtue or form or necessity, reveals itself to be more destructive and false than either evil or innocence. The Captain, a man morally and intellectually as well as practically vicious, indeed belongs most of all outside the dialectic of a humane society. For such viciousness convinced of its virtue is incorrigible.

Unfortunately, such captains provide the forms and the powers of the warship world and the actual society. One must either eliminate the vicious virtue or redefine politics. Perhaps we can pose the perplexity this way: Who or what could replace Vere? Melville's treatment of his fable makes Vere into a Dostoyevskian Grand Inquisitor. This allows no liberal amelioration and blocks the usual political antitheses. In neither practice nor principle could one conceive innocence or evil, Budd or Claggart, properly taking command from Vere. Command itself must go. No mutinous alternative even tangentially exists. The present authority, an "exceptional" man, apparently represents the best the accepted order can produce. (The unique possibility, represented in the digression on Nelson, suffers the necessary brevity and fatality of the high heroic.) One can sympathize with the philosopher who wants to find in the politically charged fable of *Billy Budd* a practical political choice. Vere obviously seems the only one, if we could somehow justify his doing the work of evil and destroying innocence.

But when such authority also resides in bad arguments and dubious if not mad motives, and maintains only injustice and repression, and ends with pathetic and futile results, the problem becomes desperate, the arguments fantastic. Thus Arendt seems driven to assert that the law in general "cannot but punish elemental goodness."[34] As harsh as Vere's rationalizations, this can only end in viciousness. The practical moralist might counter that even if the law could not be sufficiently responsive to reward the innocent for accidentally killing an evil man engaged in a crime, it could at least be sufficiently humane to let him off (with a nominal manslaughter charge and "mercy"?), thus maintaining the forms but not killing the spirit of the law, or murdering the man. If law lacks such human responsiveness, then all lasting institutions of law should be in doubt. And indeed they must be, for Captain Vere goes beyond violating naval law in defending it and more generally represents the lawful order. Since Melville makes clear that Vere, however mad, stands superior to other officers, then the question does not just lie with the captain-judge, or with the substitution of another captain-judge within the same institutional order. The question must cut deeper: If the law cannot restrain evil but only carry out its destruction of innocence, then what justification for the law?

If lawful order be so false and destructive, then crime—by definition the exceptional activity—must be preferable to the more-than-criminal law, simply as a prudent calculus. The cynic is justified in preferring the irregularities of crime to the inhumanities of the rigorous use of the law. Now, let us grant that the political philosopher such as Arendt may not really mean what she says, that the law must kill goodness, only the truism that the saints and the like are troublesome. But Melville's Vere does mean what he says and kills what he believes to be a complete innocent, a very "angel," and the philosopher's argument defends this. We might reasonably choose to reject the entire legitimacy of lawful order if its object be to destroy the innocent or the good or the holy or the heroic or even just the peculiar. The practical moral would be to feel no obligation to "lasting

---

[34]All Arendt citations are from the passages previously quoted. For bringing *On Revolution* to my attention, and for detailed argument defending Arendt's views, I am much indebted to a political philosopher, Professor Elbridge Rand of the University of British Columbia.

institutions," and the more their endurance the less the acquiescence in their existence. As prudent human beings, we might well prefer chaos to the thoroughly anti-human, or disorder to death camps, or primitive society to a dehumanized "civilization," or no navy rather than that of the Captain Veres. If these be the choices, one might reasonably prefer going quite beyond politics.

As I understand *Billy Budd*, this is where the logic of Melville's position leads. The issue gets further complicated in an essentially conservative emphasis Melville reveals in spite of the drastic implications.[35] Even "ironist" interpretations should admit this. For however mocking or inverted Melville's treatment of his subject, his response also remains conservative, limiting, in the perception of social possibility or political choice. While he shows authority and order, as with Vere's warship world, as essentially false reason and "brute force," he certainly allows little possibility to the revolutionary alternatives, such as French revolutionary victory or British mutiny. Much evidence against reforming or radical upheaval could be cited from Melville's other writings. The neatest might be his epitomization of a small version of a revolutionary regime: "Permanent Riotocracy."[36]

[35]The view has been most flatly stated by Richard Chase: the Burkean *Billy Budd* "dramatizes the conservative idea that society must follow a middle way of expediency and compromise." The "implied lesson" is that the "appropriate virtues . . . are resignation and stoic forbearance." *The American Novel and Its Tradition* (New York, 1957), p. 114. In partial contrast is a recent study I came upon after finishing my argument. It recognizes some of the savaging reversal I have emphasized: "The appalling truth of *Billy Budd* is not that innocence must be sacrificed to maintain the order of the world, but rather that innocence is destroyed by the forces of chaos and darkness masquerading as 'measured forms'." Edgar A. Dryden, *Melville's Thematics of Form* (Baltimore, 1968), p. 268.

[36]This is applied by Melville to the mutinous regime of naval deserters in Sketch Seven of the "Encantadas," *The Complete Stories of Herman Melville*, ed. Jay Leyda (New York, 1949), p. 84. In a number of these stories Melville's manner might be described as jocularly conservative (suitable to his magazine audience?). Other statements of Melville's on rebellious upheaval, though not the above, are given by Hayford and Sealts, "Notes and Commentary," pp. 195 ff.

In confirmation of that conservative temper, we might also note the politics suggested in material apparently cancelled from *Billy Budd* and printed in earlier editions as the Preface.[37] There the narrator comments on the revolutionary times in which the story takes place: "Straight away the Revolution itself became a wrongdoer, one more oppressive than the kings." Melville suggests no doubts about this orthodox view of revolutions as self-devouring. However, the description is not as self-evident as Melville, and the others who quote this passage, seem to assume. Does the relatively short and emphatic injustice of the revolutionary upheaval add up to more injustice than the enduring falsities and cruelties and repressions of the old regime? Only, I suspect, if a trauma is always taken as more pain than a permanent infection, a wound as more suffering than general debility.[38] For such conclusions, the arithmetic of misery as well as the awareness of human repression must often be quite inadequate.

Melville adds the cautious qualification to the above statement that the "outcome of it all [the revolution and its consequences] would be what to some thinkers it has since turned out to be, a political advance along nearly the whole line for Europeans." The manner here is not without Melville's usual ambiguities ("some thinkers"?), but generally serves a conservative view. Revolutions, of course, can never be chosen in terms of consequences only; anything that radical must stake itself against historical odds, risk defeat and tragic price for more immediate imperatives. Furthermore, the advances in Europe Melville

---

[37] The Preface still appears in most editions and anthologized versions of the story. I cite it from a reprint of the Plomer text (London, 1946), *Herman Melville: Four Short Novels* (New York, 1959), p. 197. I incidentally attempt to suggest why it might not fit Melville's final view of his fable.

[38] The conventional miscalculations of the cost of revolution as against the cost of the status quo are partly examined by Barrington Moore, Jr., *The Social Origins of Dictatorship and Democracy* (New York, 1967). That he too readily assumes the positive values of "modernization" and the politics of technocracy does not deny his more general point on revolutionary change.

seems to be pointing to can equally well be attributed not to the revolution but to its countering or amelioration or failure. (Liberal critics may have been misled as to the political significance of such passages as this because of the moderation that contrasts with the dogmatic reaction of Vere to what was going on "across the Channel.") Finally, if Melville did drop this redemption-by-establishment view of the Revolution from *Billy Budd* that would be appropriate in that the effects of revolution show little relevance to a fable which denies any truth from suffering and allows for no revolt.

A second passage from the same material of Melville's might be considered here. Melville discusses mutiny as similar to revolution. Though conservatives usually merge the two—I suppose out of fear—and their policies often force rebellions to become revolutions, revolutionaries usually see them as quite separate and often as antithetical. Mutinies, and similar rebellious actions, rarely pose a new order, found a new navy or social system, unlike most modern revolutions. The young Herman Melville showed, so far as I can find, no sense of revolution but did apparently engage in mutinous behavior and deserted cruel shipmasters. Such rebellion appears in his fictions as positive. Much sailor discontent receives empathetic portrayal from ex-sailor Melville, and he justifies it with considerable fervency in his account of a year as a common seaman aboard a U. S. warship, *White Jacket*.[39] Probably the most clearly heroic figure in all of Melville's work is Steelkilt in *Moby Dick*, the proudly handsome sailor who creates a violent and fully justified mutiny, happily sees the evil mate killed by the whale, and, shrewdly successful rebel,

---

[39]The contrasting final paragraph of *White Jacket* is sometimes cited to refute the rebellious emphasis in Melville's earlier writings. He concludes that "we the people suffer many abuses" but "each man must be his own savior. For the rest, whatever befall us, let us never train our murderous guns inboard; let us not mutiny with bloody pikes in our hands." Is Melville always this fearful about doing anything against a vicious order, or is this merely the sententious placebo ending for a semi-protest novel by a popular author? The evidence is not conclusive, but, either way, Melville tends to be *consciously* conservative.

escapes.[40] Some imaginative proximity in Melville to such rebels might be traced through other of his writings, even to the germinal notion of *Billy Budd* as a study of a mutinous sailor. But *Billy Budd* contains no rebel. The entitling *naif* is not even an unconscious rebel since he seems quite incapable of refusal, horrified at defiance and mutiny, and really defeated by his submissiveness. In *Billy Budd* any sympathy of Melville's for rebels gets fully displaced by his more nihilistic theme which demands an innocent, not a rebel.

The Great Mutiny of thousands of British sailors at the Nore, ruthlessly put down in the same year in which Melville places his story, provides explicit background to *Billy Budd* and hovers around it yet never enters in except as the ideological paranoia of authority, the completely unsubstantiated and apparently quite unjustified fears of the Captain. Curious that no mutinous feeling and action appear aboard the *Bellipotent* under the rigid Vere and the harsh mistreatment of the enslaved sailors. But no mutinous touch, except in Claggart's lies, appears, whether because of Melville's mockery of the false fears of Vere or because of a failure of his art.[41] In that cancelled material for *Billy Budd*, previously quoted, Melville condemns the mutiny of the Nore for "inordinate and aggressive demands." He also draws a conservative moral: "Yet in a way analogous to the operation of the Revolution at large, the Great Mutiny, though by Englishmen naturally deemed monstrous at the time, doubtless gave the first latent promptings to most important reforms in the British Navy."

Almost everything Melville says in that passage seems

[40]The point is suggested by Harry Levin's description of the rebel here as Melville's "most authentic hero." *The Power of Blackness* (New York, 1958), p. 216.

[41]Leslie Fiedler probably overstates the case for viewing *Billy Budd* as expression of Melville's loss of literary virility and his collapse into the melodramatic and sentimental. *Love and Death in the American Novel*, rev. ed. (New York, 1966), p. 454.

extremely dubious, from the description of the mutiny through the analogizing with revolution to the claimed prompting of reforms. In fact, the most obvious candidate for reform, flogging (an example appears in *Billy Budd*) was not officially removed for another three generations (1879) and so hardly suggests much effect of the Great Mutiny. Even that, and most of the other nineteenth-century reforms, can far better be explained in terms of the British Navy slowly catching up with changed conditions and attitudes in the society at large. As historical moralizer, Melville seems quite obtuse.

Certainly no one in the story sees the Budd episode as in anyway related to arbitrary and cruel authority meriting reform. Not a word of such ameliorations is mentioned. Whether the nihilistic view implicit in Melville's treatment of the story or the moderate conservative view explicit in the excluded material most fully represents the attitude of the aged Melville cannot easily be determined. The conservative emphasis probably accords with the orthodoxies of his time, with the probable effects on the man of his years as a little government official, and with his historical sources for *Billy Budd*.[42] Yet the exclusion of the "preface" and the whole bent of the story suggests something more extreme. Perhaps consciously Melville would be a conservative; in dialectical and imaginative fact, he is a nihilist.

As I read the modern accounts of the Great Mutiny (some of which take views similar to Melville's conservative statements), it was more than justified.[43] The mutineers may reasonably be judged as impractically and immorally moderate, and not at all sufficiently "inordinate and aggressive." Their demands were excellent but defeated by unjustified restraint. Following the

[42]Hayford and Sealts cite evidence for Melville's use of William James, *Naval History of Great Britain*, 6 vols. (London, 1859). The passages from it available to me, as cited in other histories, indicate a bigoted officialese view of the mutinies.

[43]My main source here is the most recent and detailed account of the mutinies, James Dugan, *The Great Mutiny* (New York, 1965). He does not make the same interpretation of the mutiny that I suggest. See also Bonamy Dobree and G. E. Manwaring, *The Floating Republic* (London, 1935).

lead of the elected president of the mutineers, the exceptionally decent Richard Parker,[44] they made no effort to kill their foul officers and even insisted on sobriety and politeness. In historical perspective it seems easy to plot the double failure of the Great Mutiny, though we can hardly blame the mutineers for a decency far greater than that of their officers and government or for mistakenly following the pattern of the earlier Spithead Mutiny which had resulted in some, though quite insufficient, redress of grievances. Hardly any of the mutineers, it seems, attempted revolution by combining with Jacobin elements and the widespread discontent on land against the corrupt and cruel British autocracy.[45] Even as pure mutiny, the Nore rebellion was not carried very far and little effort was made to destroy the ships and flee, which might well have been the most sensible and moral action.

Perhaps implicitly, Melville's portrayal of the loyally submissive Budd and the timorous crew of the *Bellipotent* does suggest some unmanly quality or ideological victimization of British sailors which terribly limited their ability to adequately rebel against cruel and contemptible authority. Is it Melville's own assumption that one would "naturally" consider disruption of the British Navy as "monstrous"? Perhaps, for his other works display some of the usual American literateur's Anglophilism. However, the modern reader could well find such a prejudice at best unthoughtful and be led to speculate on what a positive contribution to a history of liberty the destruction of British

[44]See Dugan, pp. 329-352.

[45]E. P. Thompson, *The Making of the English Working Class* (New York, 1964), several times suggests that the mutinies were really at one with the Jacobin revolutionary movement. Dugan counters (p. 463) that there is no specific evidence for this conclusion. My separation of the mutiny and the revolution assumes a considerable difference, normally, between rebellion and revolution, which seems confirmed by the descriptions of the behavior of the British mutineers. The fallacy which I think revolutionary ideologues tend to impose is to see rebellion as merely a phase moving toward revolution rather than rebellion as an end in itself—and often quite justified as just that. Contemporary as well as historical rebellions could be cited in support.

power in 1797 could have been. Here, as elsewhere, Melville's rhetoric takes such an essentially conservative cast that no mere irony can altogether qualify it. Melville's irony, then, is rarely corrective but often, as in *Billy Budd,* Pyrrhic.[46] The logic of such despair leads to a conservative nihilism.

Such interpreters as Arendt altogether miss this crucial quality, in politics as well as in art. She, instead, wants us to accept several destructive myths as the basis of politics: Societies are "founded" by Cains, and therefore properly continued by Veres. And, quoting Vere's rationalization, the welfare of mankind can be maintained only by the formal pretenses to "lasting institutions," no matter at what cost of falsity, evil and destruction. But Pyrrhic Melville's treatment of his fable will not allow this contention, in spite of his substitution of an untenable innocence for rebellion. No latent improvements, no admirable behavior, no significant and enduring myths, no Orphean music, no lasting good for mankind, results from the institutions that kill evil Claggart, innocent Budd and viciously virtuous Vere. We must either despair or conclude that such institutions should not last—or do both.

In one of the more obscure epilogues to *Billy Budd,* the inconclusive discussion of the Purser and Surgeon, an ancient concept of "euthanasia" as a willed and pleasurable suicide (a rather Schopenhauerish notion) comes up as explanation for the passive death of Billy Budd. Here, similar to what we shall find in his earlier fables, we see a bitter and despairing Melville. Only an absolute refusal, a total resistance, would seem relevant, though it does not directly appear in *Billy Budd.* True, the warship world presented by Melville defines the human condition as nearly hopeless, and often suggests a merely ruminative resigna-

[46]Irony, like satire, is more often politically and morally conservative of the present order than revolutionary. Of course there are notable exceptions (Zamiatin and the "permanent revolution" at the heart of *We,* in contrast to conservative Swift, etc.). Such negative and despairing irony as Melville's shows little evidence of an intentionally liberating direction, though some of the implications may finally be quite different.

tion. Whether Melville "intended" to express this or not makes little difference. That is what is there. We feel driven to the outside edge, beyond politics, beyond myth, finally outside any assertion of human value where artistic coherence can hardly contain the nihilistic response.

Melville's nihilistic fable, then, does not provide a paradigm of political choice but of its denial. It does, however, provide the broadly relevant political-moral "test." The case of Billy Budd suggests that any social order must be judged on what it does to those outside or beyond political response: the children and the old, the slaves and the barbarians, the unpropertied and the uneducated, the saints and the innocents. If the authorities justify whipping the kids, repressing the lively, exploiting the subject, locking up the aged, mistreating the minorities, or any of the other ways of hanging the innocent, we see the essential dynamism of that order. The psychic core as well as the real politics become exposed at the non-political edges. There we discover the order's legitimacy or, as with the *Bellipotent,* its illegitimacy. It is an order without justification.

The British warship and its autocratic empire, the "measured forms" and the King's buttons, the "lasting institutions" and their twisted myths—these are the products of false consciousness. The existential choices must be against them. Our concern should focus not on the justifying mythologies but on the individual humaneness. What are those institutions that hang the darling Billys really doing? Their claims to enduring beneficence turn out, on existential analysis, to be mad mystification. The "case of Billy Budd" reveals itself as no mere incident but as the nuclear experience of that law and order. We do not excuse part-time sadists from our horror, rightly suspecting most else that they do. No more can we excuse the Veres' aberrations from our horror, rightly realizing that it characterizes most else that they do. The very "inevitability" and "reasonableness" of the hanging of Billy Budd, so fully acquiesced in by a majority of the commentators, confirms our choice of rejecting the warship world. An order which essentially empowers the malignant and kills the innocent and legitimizes this with false claims to virtue, this is evil and should be refused. That is the existential moral and political choice.

Did Melville "intend" this? The tale, and his sustained conservative nihilism, allow no affirmation of what is. Granted, this does not take the hopefully libertarian directions some of us might prefer. But the story drastically undercuts rather than glorifying "brute force" and authoritarianism's delusions of tragic grandeur and most claims in the name of "lasting institutions." Nothing less than the will to resistance will make sense of human choice in an order of malignant policemen and submissive innocents and vicious virtues. Otherwise we repeat Cain's crime to pseudo-Orphean martial music. *Billy Budd,* then, argues that politics must be the rejection of the crimes of politics. In other words, down with "lasting institutions"!

Melville mostly laments the bitterness of it all, while providing insights into the existential choices that must be made. Though he proposes no alternative actions, his art insists we not be fooled into taking such a world as a good one.[47] This annihilating awareness goes quite beyond politics, but it also wisely and radically informs us for the locally human refusals.

[47] J. E. Oates points to the "Timonism" that runs through much of the later Melville and to this story as "an expression of negation." "Melville and the Manichean Illusion," *Texas Studies in Literature and Language,* IV Spring 1962), pp. 117-129. But much of this nihilism (why the euphemistic Timonism?) may also be found in the earlier Melville, as in the comment in *Moby Dick* that this is "a wicked, miserable world," p. 460.

★

CHAPTER THREE

BENITO CERENO
AND THE DARKNESS
OF ANNIHILATION

1. *The Logic of Despair*

Some of the significance of Melville's *Benito Cereno*,[1] another fable of destructive authority and sacrificial death and nihilistic implication, may be suggested by an existential perspective on "dread." The failure adequately to recognise such concern provides much of the issue in Melville's stories. In *Benito Cereno*, a polished melodrama, the problem centers on an American Captain, Amasa Delano, whose merchant ship is anchored at a desert island off the South American coast. Seeing a strange ship in trouble, he goes to aid it and spends the day on board with the apparently debilitated Spanish Captain, Benito Cereno, and his cargo of black slaves. In spite of obscure dreads, which he energetically resists, the American discovers only as he leaves the immediate cause of the peculiar behavior of Captain Cereno,

---

[1] All otherwise unidentified citations are to "Benito Cereno" in *The Complete Stories of Herman Melville*, ed. Jay Leyda (New York, 1949), pp. 255-354. Because of many brief quotations, individual page numbers are not given. There does not seem to be any significant textual problem in this story. For the minor variations between the first periodical publication and the first book publication, see the annotations in *A Benito Cereno Handbook*, ed. Seymour L. Gross (Belmont, Calif., 1965), pp. 1-70. I also draw upon some of the critical material in this collection. A parallel but less adequate collection is *Melville's "Benito Cereno": A Text For Guided Research*, ed. John P. Runden (Boston, 1964).

the ominously solicitous blacks and the badly disordered ship. It turns out that the Spanish Captain is a prisoner, following a slave revolt, and that the blacks have elaborately masqueraded their power in order to fool the American and capture his ship. Cereno and Delano escape, the Americans attack and capture the rebel slaves and take them to Peru for trial and cruel punishment. To the American Captain's continuing perplexity, Captain Cereno, though saved from the slaves and masquerade, withdraws from active life and soon dies. Whether impelled by remorse, bitterness, or Christian renunciation seems unclear, but he has reached an overwhelming despair that defeats life.

What seems applicable here is the major existentialist view of the meaning of despair. A philosopher has summarized it as follows:

The decisive character of dread is that it cannot be localized and it refuses to be pinned down to anything in which we are interested and which we feel to be threatened by emptying everything in the world of all interest for me, it invests everything alike with a common worthlessness . . . . what inspires my dread is recognition of what it means to-be-in-the-world, when I see this in its totality and not merely in the perspectives of my particular preoccupations . . . . dread . . . isolates me in this recognition that I can either continue this impersonally determined inauthentic existence or by heroic effort take personal charge of my own existence. . . . Thus dread which at first in contrast to fear is so vague and meaningless proves the most specific and significant of all emotions, a pitiless pointing to my original situation . . . and a fear for my authenticity in living. . . .

Personal existence, being always what it will be, never simply and solely what it is, has no finality and totality of its own and is never achieved. When death supervenes its possibilities are extinguished but not exhausted. Moreover, death does not strike me down, it is not an accident which happens to me, it is from the very beginning one of my own possibilities which I nurse within me. Indeed, it *is* my possibility eminently, because its realization is inevitable and will be realized by me in the most authentically personal way without any possibility of avoidance or substitution . . . . If I can die, I need not have existed, nobody need exist, personal existence is launched between nothingness and nothingness and it is nothingness that is real, everything is absurd, the impossibility of existence is possible, nothing is necessary . . . . dread reveals to me . . . that I am cast into the world to die there. This is the truth of our situation which is hidden from us by our daily preoccupations and by the authority of the impersonal mode of social existence. . . .

Death, then, is the clue to authentic living, the eventual and omnipresent possibility which binds together and stabilizes my existence. . . . I anticipate death not by suicide but by living in the presence of death as always immediately possible and as undermining everything. This full-blooded acceptance *(amor fati)* of death, lived out, is authentic personal existence. . . . In face of this capital possibility which devours all the others, there are only two alternatives: acceptance or distraction. Even this choice is a rare privilege, since few are awakened by dread to the recognition of the choice, most remain lost in the illusions of everyday life. To choose acceptance of death as the supreme and normative possibility of my existence is not to reject the world and refuse participation in its daily preoccupations, it is to refuse to be deceived and to refuse to be identified with the preoccupations in which I engage: it is to take them for what they are worth—nothing. From this detachment springs the power, the dignity, the tolerance of authentic personal existence.[2]

[2]H. J. Blackham, *Six Existentialist Thinkers* (New York, 1959), pp. 94-97. I have abbreviated the passage. In an effort at reasonable clarity, I have used this paraphrase of Martin Heidegger's *Sein und Zeit* (1927). See *Being and Time* (London, 1962), pp. 279-311. While some of Blackham's adaption may be questionable as a statement of Heidegger, it makes some points of value in themselves. As I understand Heidegger, awareness of death in an authentic way should lead to a heightening of subjectivity in which one reaches "understanding of one's ownmost and uttermost potentiality-for-Being" (p. 310). While the basic notions, and some of the ponderousness, may derive from Soren Kierkegaard's *Concept of Dread,* it seems likely that the key insight is drawn from Tolstoy's *Death of Ivan Ilyich,* which I therefore draw upon for the continuation of the discussion, below.

No one in *Benito Cereno* appears adequately to achieve such awareness of being-in-the-world, the perspective through dread and beyond practical preoccupation and the impersonal social mode, to reach an authentic life style. But the issue is pervasively present in the images of darkness and despair and death, mockingly masqueraded, throughout the story. The "good Captain," optimistic American and Melville's recurrent portrait of the benevolent rationalist, remains obtuse, preoccupied with the practical, not knowing that he despairs and therefore not understanding what happens around him. Even in drastic danger aboard the Spanish slave ship, he denies the possibility of his own death and never allows for that of others, and he therefore suffers, in Heidegger's terms, "a constant tranquilization about death."[3] The "bad Captain," decadent and traditionally religious European and also Melville's recurrent victim of evil, knows he despairs but with false logic blames it, as his social role demands, on the devilish black man who led the revolt and conjured the terrifying masquerade around death. He falsifies and destroys his own being by, as Heidegger puts it, the fallacious objectification and externalization of non-existence and "brooding on death."[4] With some of Melville's usual irony, the partly aware man despairingly dies while the unaware lives on in false assurance, but neither achieves "freedom towards death."[5] Those who do not have freedom cannot, of course, give it to others. The death-dealing—and finally death's-head representation of life— of the black slaves provides the dominating image of the story. The failure of authenticity furthers rather than cauterizes the black despair that obsessed Melville and provided the dialectic of his dark art.

The blackness of dread takes several forms, several masquerades, in *Benito Cereno,* but finally reveals the despair over human

[3]*Being and Time,* p. 290.

[4]*Being and Time,* p. 305.

[5]*Being and Time,* p. 311. Melville's critics do not usually make much of the death issue and the related consciousness.

nothingness, of which death is the most relentless reality. To Captain Cereno, in his final conversation with Captain Delano, the Negro rebel-slave leader Babo, who casts the shadow over the Spaniard's unmanned white consciousness, suggests, as he literally becomes after his execution, a death-head overseeing all. No pleasant nature nor practical concern, as both avowed and represented by the genial American, can banish the blackness as the dominant truth. Nature has neither memory nor humanity, Cereno replies to the American's moral placebos, and so cannot provide any real solace. The warm breezes do not come with a "human-like healing" to those really aware that "they but waft me to my tomb." In *Benito Cereno,* as well as in other works, Melville may be seen as a forerunner and practitioner of modern existentialist consciousness. Perhaps most crucial to this perspective is the insistence that despair over the blackness of existence shall not be denied.

2. *The Blacks*

Within this existential concern with dread we find a specific but pervasive social issue, the blackness of our white consciousness we call "the Negro problem." Its relative importance to *Benito Cereno* provides focus for considerable disagreement. Many commentators, at least until recent years, considered the Negro in the story only in terms of the other literary motifs, such as appearance versus reality and awareness of evil versus benevolent rationalism. But such "classic" literary motifs do not exist as things in themselves; they would be mere literary technology if not based in the anguished awareness of human mortality. To speak of the disparities of appearances and realities—whether in Shakespeare or in Melville—becomes empty gesture if not related to why we find them in conflict, why man must take up false appearances to hide from himself the annihilating realities.

Babo, the leader of the revolting black slaves, *appears* benevolent to the rationalizing good American Captain because Delano must refuse to recognize fully the meaning of human slavery and the revenge it engenders. Melville's motif of appearance versus reality then serves as an exploration of death-denying and evil-denying American false consciousness. To simply use the old literary motif of appearance-reality would mean to play with a conundrum in which the reality of literature is reduced to its appearances, but we must ask the moral questions. The contemporary American reader, sensitive to our historic crimes of slavery and exploitation, and our continuing racism and mistreatment of blacks, reasonably asks of such literature as *Benito Cereno:* What attitude does it show towards slavery and racist consciousness, and all the viciousness that they encouraged?[6]

As is usual with Melville, parts of the answer tend to be ambiguous. The blacks came finally to symbolize a metaphysical curse, the white hatred of the dark side of sensibility, the blackness of death and nothingness that we would deny. But along the way to that representation in the story appear at least three views of the Negro. Yankee Captain Delano originally shows a blandly patronizing view of the blacks and a "half-gamesome" banter in which he "took to negroes . . . just as other men to Newfoundland dogs." He considers the black men "indisputable inferiors," "stupid," "natural servants," created to be submissive, musical, and amusing in the "docility arising from the unaspiring contentment of a limited mind." These images of Delano's belong to the tradition of the minstrel show "darky."[7] Melville clearly mocks this grossly blind stereotype and self-congratulating prejudice. For Delano's genial-darky view leads him to almost fatally

[6]I grant my own ambivalences here. When I first wrote a discussion of *Benito Cereno,* twenty years ago, I gave the "Negro problem" a paragraph. By the middle sixties that had grown to six pages, as is evident in my article on the story in *Studies in Short Fiction,* V (Spring 1968), pp. 225-238. Similarly, it has been pointed out to me that in an article some years ago on Richard Wright—see "The Existential Darkness: Richard Wright's *The Outsider,*" *Five Black Writers* (New York, 1970)—I never even mentioned that the author was black.

[7]Leslie A. Fiedler draws the parallel with the minstrel show "black-faced Sambo" but does not give other consideration to the work, which he judges a theatrical "gothic horror tale." *Love and Death in the American Novel,* rev. ed. (New York, 1966), pp. 400-401.

misjudge, and even wish to purchase as an ideal personal slave, the murderous Babo. (Incidentally, the name probably does not derive from "baboon," as has been suggested by several scholars,[8] but seems to be a variant of the derisive "babu"—originally a Hindu form of polite address adapted as a generic term for "native" by Anglo-American sailors and later replaced by such still current insulting Americanisms as "gook."[9]) By grace of his bigotry, Delano quite misconstrues the mutinous slaves and their masquerade. Here Melville may suggest that the worst bigotries, those least open to an awareness of reality, are the most ostensibly kindly ones.

In sharp antithesis to the Yankee's good-darky view of the Africans, which works out not to be so consistent as to deter him from ordering later on a murderous assault against them, is the black reaction of Don Benito Cereno. He sees the blacks as only "malign," as dehumanized pure evil. Even after the revolt is squashed, Captain Cereno will not go on the deck of the American ship while little Babo, a tied-up prisoner, remains there. Cereno refuses to identify Babo for the court which tries the rebel slaves, or even to look at him, and he faints when pressed to do so. Even with Babo condemned to death, Cereno stays obsessed with his revulsive fear of the blacks. His final words in the story—in answer to Delano's question, "What has cast such a shadow upon you?"—are simply "The negro." He apparently renounces life, for a monastery and then for death, because of his terror of evil represented by black Babo. Benito Cereno's responses, fully linked by Melville with the imagery and allu-

[8]This has become established in the scholarship, apparently following the arbitrary associations of Stanley T. Williams, "Follow Your Leader: Melville's 'Benito Cereno'," *Virginia Quarterly Review*, XXII (Winter 1947), pp. 65-76.

[9]The far-fetched efforts at associational readings—often called "symbolism" in the classroom—include "the name 'Babo' being possibly a variant of the Tuscan 'Babbo,' meaning 'Daddy'." Robert Magowan, "Masque and Symbol in Melville's *Benito Cereno*," *College English*, XXIII (February 1962), p. 349 (note). The derisive cognate for "native" may be found in most dictionaries of slang; I first found, but did not record, it in a sailor autobiography.

sions of religious renunciation, seem obsessional and unrecognized guilt. Certainly Don Benito shows no direct acknowledgment of his own role and blackness as a rich slave master. A proper victim of a justified, though excessively cruel, slave revolt and attempted flight to freedom, Cereno—and perhaps his author, who quite minimizes Cereno's nasty role—fails in awareness of evil, an evil made even uglier by his gestures of gentlemanly sensitivity and Christian piety.

A third view of the Negro may surface in some curious details of the novella. The final description of Babo, for example, does not seem to fit either Cereno or Delano—guilty morbidity or genial bigotry. Babo, willfully silent forever after his capture, gives no explanation of himself as a maritime Nat Turner, and Melville only externally shows his remarkable intelligence and courage. Yet his superior head provides the final image of the story: "for many days, the head, that hive of subtlety, fixed on a pole in the Plaza, met, unabashed, the gaze of the whites. . . ." And that deathhead, Melville tells us, points past the grave of his former master, Aranda (killed by Babo) towards Mount Agonia, where his last "master," Don Benito Cereno, soon dies. "Benito Cereno, borne on the bier, did, indeed, follow his leader." "Follow your leader" is what Babo chalked above the bones of slave-master Aranda. With macabre adjuration, Babo had fixed his master's bones as figure head for Cereno's *San Dominick* and used them and the slogan as mocking threat for the remainder of the Spaniards kept alive to run the ship back to Africa. But both on board the ship and in death we see Babo as the real leader. Does Melville imply that Babo—and by extrapolation, all slaves—lead masters like Cereno towards guilty renunciation of life?

Certainly the final scene of the story might be viewed as the slave mastering the enslaver in death. The slave leader's stoic silence and defiant end, qualities usually treated as admirable virtues by Melville, suggest heroic dimensions to go with his diabolical cleverness in capturing the Spanish ship and in developing an elaborate masquerade which successfully misleads the American captain. Such details indicate a view of the blacks difficult to relate to Delano's darky bigotry or to Cereno's obsessionally malignant fear. This third view of the blacks echoes in some other details of the story. For example, the giant Negro Atufal, reportedly a former African king, wears chains and padlock on the *San Dominick*. Captain Cereno carries the key to that lock on "a slender silken cord" around his neck. Ostensibly, Atufal must report every two hours to Cereno; if he asks the Spanish Captain for "pardon," the padlock will be opened and the chains struck. So the American Captain is told. Developed at ornate length, this bit of literary gothic illustrates Melville's proclivity towards melodramatic involution. Does it do something more? Delano expresses admiration for the adamant "royal spirit" of slave Atufal refusing to ask for pardon, contradicting his darky view of the blacks. He also says, "So, Don Benito—padlock and key—significant symbols, truly." But we later learn that Atufal helped lead the revolt and that his enchainment provides part of the masquerade to mislead the American. Thus Delano misreads the "symbols." In reality, he who is padlocked and chained stands, both in fact and in spirit, as the real master, while he who has the key and gestures of authority cowers in reality as the victim. The reality contradicts the masquerade, though the American congenitally refuses to recognize this.

The lock-and-key may portend yet more. Considering the emphasis on them, they may well be, in Delano's words, "significant symbols, truly." Since Melville emphasizes the contrast between the physically commanding Atufal and the passive and effete Cereno, we might also recognize an ironic implication in the usual sexual imagery of lock-and-key. The royal Negro slave, in reality rather than in the masqueraded appearance of his locked chains, represents a vital force while the trembling and effete Spanish Captain, with his silken-corded key, suffers a rape-like imposition. The bland American of the *Bachelor's Delight* must miss some of the deeper currents of relation and feeling involved here. But such an undertone, both in its subtlety and its homoeroticism, should be subordinated to the more crucial slave-master relationship established by the dramatic scene. The reversal of the lock-and-key, in terms of both authority and sexuality, mocks slavery with the master mastered. The violation of the nature of the would-be master, by his own enslaving role (whether as actual slave or actual master), illustrates one of the terrible consequences of the institution of slavery—and of the rebellion against it: to take someone else's freedom is to destroy your own freedom.

Another instance of mocking irony about Negro slavery appears in Captain Delano's comments on Francisco, the "rajah-looking mulatto" steward. To Delano's charmed eye, the steward's fine manners show him as the epitome of genteel civilization—at "once Christian and Chesterfieldian" and "king of kind hearts and polite fellows." But the reader of Melville soon learns that he delights in revealing the nasty reality under the appearance of civilization. Delano ask Cereno if the mulatto steward is not a "Good worthy fellow?" Don Benito, under the eyes of several of his black captors, can only respond affirmatively. The smugly benevolent Delano replies: "Ah, I thought so. For it were strange, indeed, and not very creditable to us white-skins, if a little of our blood mixed with the African's, should, far from improving the latter's quality, have the sad effect of pouring vitriolic acid in black broth. . . ." Melville reverses this hint with obvious dramatic irony; as we learn from the court depositions, which provide the doubling later section of the story, this fine-mannered mulatto "was one of the first hand of revolters." And just before the meal on board the Spanish vessel at which Delano made these comments, the steward "proposed, to the Negro Babo, poisoning a dish for the generous Captain Amasa Delano." The harsh reflective irony once again shows the benevolent American's imperceptiveness. But in this episode we find also, again, the sexual reversal so central to chattel slavery. The enslaving "white-skins" did indeed pour "vitriolic acid into black broth."

The sexually poisoned meal, still apparent today in the rape-paranoic fantasies of many whites as well as in the reversing blonde-chick fixation of many blacks, provides endless indigestion in the libidinal diet.[10]

As Melville's Delano rightly says at one point, though he misuses it at that moment, "Ah, this slavery breeds ugly passions in man." Thus Melville subtlely savages the institution of slavery with these astute perceptions. His irony, as some readers overlook, makes Delano's perceptions true though misapplied rather than simply reversed. However, if we were to conclude, from the analysis of such detailing as we find in these three episodes, that the "Negro question" is settled in *Benito Cereno,* our reading would be disingenuous, however subtle.

Melville's other writings do not display much of Cereno's obsessed view of the blacks as personifications of malignity. It has often been noted—and perhaps over-noted—that Melville treats blacks with somewhat more benevolence than may have been conventional in his time—specifically in *Moby Dick* and *Redburn.*[11] However, most of this nineteenth-century author's

[10]Good background material as well as analytic detail on the slavery issue may be found in Sidney Kaplan, "Herman Melville and the American National Sin: The Meaning of 'Benito Cereno'," *Journal of Negro History,* XLI (October 1956), pp. 311-338, and XLII (January 1957), pp. 11-37. While some of his details seem arguable, such as his acceptance of Williams' interpretation of Babo (p. 22), some of his emphasis on Melville's bigotry seems justified. I do not see that the recent counter-arguments change this. See Margaret M. Vanderhaar, "A Re-Examination of 'Benito Cereno'," *American Literature,* XL (May 1968), pp. 179-191. She rightly sees Delano as a complex character and Melville as against slavery (a decade later, anyway), but does not see the limitations of his opposition or his response to "blackness." Eleanor M. Simpson argues, rather unconvincingly I believe, that Melville's early treatment of blacks sometimes avoids stereotypes and that Babo is not a usual Negro stereotype, but fails to note that he is a diabolical one. "Melville and the Negro: From *Typee* to 'Benito Cereno'," *American Literature,* XLI (March 1969), pp. 19-38.

[11]Because Melville sometimes treats dark men positively, such as Ishmael's bedmate Queequeg in *Moby Dick,* the evidence is usually read in only one direction. Queequeg, however, is not American Negro. I also take the most striking witticism in defense of the black man—"as though a white man were anything more dignified than a white-washed negro"—as a shock-effect inversion which still reveals

blacks may most accurately be viewed as comic stereotypes. In principle, it seems evident from both his comments in the fictions and in his poems, Melville opposed slavery. But quite a gap exists between that general principle and treating blacks as full human beings. We find a mad black boy, an abused but perceptive Negro comic cook, a glimpse of a cocky black sailor rightly enjoying a bit of freedom in England, an admiring portrait of a black harpooner (non-African though), and miscellaneous black sailors who sometimes receive (as in *White Jacket* as well as in *Moby Dick* and *Redburn*) pleasant epithets. Melville's anger at social exploitation and oppression certainly encourages some kindness towards blacks, but the tone is more often indulgent than egalitarian. There seems to be no evidence of skeptical Melville as deeply sympathetic to the abolitionists who, whatever their specific failures, maintained the only serious moral position in mid-nineteenth century America since no other view essentially attacked the institution of slavery, much less racism.

In *Benito Cereno* Melville, writing of course for a popular magazine audience, makes the Negroes exceptionally savage and puts but little emphasis on the similar cruelty of the American sailors who even, because of malign suspicions, gratuitously kill a Spanish sailor trying to warn them away from the *San Dominick*. Drawing on his historical source, Melville has the Spanish sailors savagely attack the bound black prisoners, though he does eliminate this brutality in the Captain. While Delano stops this particular act of cruelty, he raises no objections to the horrible sentences meted out by the supposedly Christian authorities of Lima. The American, then, can be judged the archetypal "decent" citizen, genial and kind when the rules sanction it but otherwise indifferent to established domination and cruelty. So, apparently, with the author. Generally, Melville's dramatization in *Benito Cereno* shows everyone sanctioning malignity against

---

an exacerbated color consciousness. Also in *Moby Dick*, the grotesque black cook and the mad black Pip are not developed as human beings. It does of course not follow that, because Melville is a major author, he is always just or sensitive.

the blacks, but especially shows the blacks as black, indeed, with
trickery, threats, diabolism, revenge, gratuitous cruelty, rioting
rage, and perverse destruction.[12]

In presenting a subtle reading of some of the details about the
blacks, one of my purposes is to make the best possible case for
Melville on that issue. But after giving him his fullest possible
due in insight and compassion, we must still grant that the antagonist case stands stronger. The blacks appear in the story primarily within the prejudices of Delano and Cereno. The two views
complement each other. Delano, noticing a "slumbering
Negress" on the deck, thinks of the woman as "a doe in the shade
of a woodland rock." Awakened by the nuzzling of her baby,
"delightedly she caught the child up, with maternal transports,
covering it with kisses. There's naked nature, now; pure tenderness and love, thought Captain Delano, well pleased." Glancing
at the other African women, he concludes that "like most
uncivilized women, they seemed at once tender of heart and
tough of constitution. . . ." In the doe image—the same pastoral
image of truth that Melville insisted on earlier (in the passage
quoted at the beginning of this discussion from the essay on
Hawthorne)—we have an undoubted verity, but nihilistic Melville will not leave such a truth standing long. For these comments function also as Melville's mockery of those who only see
goodness in nature (and probably also one of his recurrent pokes
at bachelors' ideas of women). Those "loving as doves" black
women, we later learn from Benito Cereno's deposition to the

12A rather touching example of scholarly ambivalence on Melville and the
"Negro problem" appears in the criticism of Joseph Schiffman. In one discussion
he writes of the story, "What an indictment of slavery!" "Critical Problems in
Melville's *Benito Cereno*," *Modern Language Quarterly*, XI (September 1950),
p. 324. A decade later he concludes, "Writing in the violent decade just before the
Civil War, when panic over slave insurrections was mounting, Melville, with
characteristic ambivalence, treated slavery and the rebellion against it as a sign
of evil in the universe. In highlighting the savagery of the rebellion, Melville sul-
lied his tale with racism. . . ." *Three Shorter Novels of Herman Melville* (New
York, 1962), p. 235. (I take this last from *A Benito Cereno Handbook*, p. 128.) He
is more candid than most Melville scholars.

court, "would have tortured to death, instead of simply killing, the Spaniards," and "in the various acts of murder, they sang songs and danced" as ritual encouragement to the violence of their men. Melville thus pushes the reader to see that Captain Delano's benign notion of human nature, with its Noble Savage bias and pastoral images, will not do. As in *Billy Budd*, Melville mocks such Rousseauean views. Many similar details, first seen benignly by Delano and then presented in harshly revealing perspective by Cereno, cumulatively insist on the malignity of the blacks. Nor does Melville present, except in the involution of ironies that run against his obvious themes, any mediating perspective that would relate evil to evil, the blacks' revenge to enslavement and racism.

The imagery of black and white, light and dark—the clichés that unduly concern pietistic critics—obviously receive considerable emphasis in this story. They mostly serve the traditional warpings of white consciousness—dark and black equated with vice and evil. Granted, Melville shows less concern in this novella with the Negro in his own right than as the theatrical embodiment of the black depths of human nature, but that itself grievously mars the moral quality of the tale. The situation, explicitly defined as a revolt of black slaves against hardly admirable whites, will not bear his white-over-black moral tone. Melville here violates the very sensitivity to the dark side of life which is the theme of *Benito Cereno*.[13]

The duplicity and vengeance of the blacks become incoherent because they are unrelated to the slavery that formed and directed their actions. Certainly the revolt and masquerade that Babo led shows a self-defeating nastiness and mad involution. His capture, inconsistent with his slyness, comes about because he stupidly

[13]While one would like to sympathize with the libertarian bias of John Bernstein, his too simple approach to Melville's art does not allow it. He sees no malignity in Babo and concludes that "Melville's tale is a warning to America to . . . 'Keep faith with the blacks. . .'." *Pacifism and Rebellion in the Writings of Herman Melville* (The Hague, Netherlands, 1964), p. 173.

leaps into Delano's boat solely to kill the escaping Cereno. The blacks lack development beyond their theatrical roles as comically disguised evil. While some of this could itself reflect the enslaving situation, Melville makes little effort to elaborate that truth. In a story so deeply involved in slavery and so subtle in its moral analysis of the American's character, the failure to grant full human nature to those who revolt against it goes beyond artistic lacunae. Even giving maximum weight to ironic suggestions, Melville's obsessive treatment of the black side of human nature as equated with the blacks reveals a moral and artistic darkness in the author. Presented at a time when the viciousness of black enslavement was well recognized, the melodrama insists on deep fears and hatreds in Melville's white consciousness.[14]

White religion may be the crux of such racial illness, as suggested by the many allusions to Christian renunciation. *Benito Cereno* arises from the Manichean even more fully than most American melodrama does.[15] Not only do we have black as evil and white as Christian goodness, as in most of our popular mythologies, but darkness takes on superlative powers, transcendent and tempting, which pervade and master all. Melville's imagination, in other works as well as here, often seems trapped within the Manichean-Christian madness, especially in its Calvinist cast out of which arose much of his, and America's, torment. In the inverted Calvinism of *Moby Dick* his Manichean imagination demonically twisted the antinomies so that in the annihilating whiteness of the superlative monster we find the

[14]Some readers mistake their urbane consciousness of the slavery issue for Melville's. See, for example, the curious argument that since all the views of slavery presented in the story are wrong, they end up "making a truth." R. W. B. Lewis, *Trials of the Word* (New Haven, Conn., 1965), p. 49. Such a casuistry can be used to justify anything at all.

[15]Some black writers now note the Manichean madness in white consciousness. See, for example, Frantz Fanon, *The Wretched of the Earth* (New York, 1968), p. 41. Fanon, of course, goes on to his own Manichean mystique of therapeutic black violence.

ambiguous malignity of the universe. The pursuit of the great white father-god becomes a black art of nihilistic heroism. In *Benito Cereno* we see a less heroic, and more nastily commonplace, piety towards the evil principle.

A century later than Melville's story, James Baldwin tells of a visit to a Swiss-Protestant village in which a black man appeared as an exotic and unique stranger. The sweet little Christian children who saw him in the village street fled screaming from what they took to be the devil.[16] Not accidentally, then, Melville's black little slave leader becomes a very devil in the fable. And by the same implacable logic of the white psyche, the unmanned Don Benito sees the Negro as the ultimate image of terror. As Melville's melodrama and imagery suggest—probably an unintentional insight—the hatred and fear and inverted worship of the dark powers and any black personification of them runs so deep in our Christian colored culture that few altogether escape them, including Melville and many of his readers.

Arguments against recognizing this sad truth about Melville run the risk of being self-serving. There is not much logic in the view that a "great artist" cannot be bigoted or that a subtle and sensitive mind cannot also be an unjust and warped one. More generally, we must recognize in our cultural heritage the considerable truth of the claims of contemporary Afro-Americans about "white racism." Our culture is pervaded by the supporting and engendering false consciousness. Exploitation deriving from the slavery legacy and the competitive socio-economic ordering carry out the cosmic drama of black and white. The imperatives to domination and repression seem inseparable from our puritan and evangelical heritages. The religious dimensions repeatedly appear in our literature. For example, in probably the most devestating dramatization of the American Protestant ethos, William Faulkner's *Light in August,* the Calvinistic characters lust for someone to castrate and crucify, preferably a black man.

---

[16]James Baldwin, "Stranger in the Village," *Notes of a Native Son* (New York, 1964), pp. 135 ff. The urban decline of Christianity, of course, helps reduce the bigotry.

Faulkner presents the twisted sexuality, the compulsive laboring, the mania for violence rather than pleasure, and the unbearable guilt. His impotent and outcast minister-intellectual concludes: *"And so why should not their religion drive them to crucifixion of themselves and one another?"*[17]

Probably Melville is not conscious of presenting a related perception of the American reality, of the mad metaphors of black and white "blood." His *Benito Cereno* seems rather more religious Southern gentleman than South American mariner. But we need not insist on this surrogate process to sense the black mania. "Prejudice" quite inadequately describes this black-white psychomachia in our civilization and the fears and guilts and hatreds represented to many more than Don Benito by "the negro" and his dark shadow. Mere social amelioration will hardly be sufficient to eliminate this burden. Melville's forlorn symbolism of the black deathhead, and of yet another anguished white master's bier being carried from Mount Agonia, shows the horrors of our white consciousness. "White racism," like stubbornly recurring anti-Semitism, may never be adequately surpassed so long as our traditional Christian-colored consciousness continues. Melville's art in *Benito Cereno* testifies to our enslaving Manicheanism. Our contemporary black militants underestimate the issue if they think only political and economic revolution, however justified and desirable those may be, can sufficiently purge our white culture of its crucifyingly destructive powers of darkness. The religious depths of that problem no doubt demand extremity, the disproportions of deconversion experiences, to bring into the dark light our nihilistic dread.

3. *The Good American*

As with *Bartleby* and *Billy Budd,* the primary dramatic focus of *Benito Cereno* belongs not to the entitling victim but to the

---

[17] William Faulkner, *Light in August* (New York, 1950), p. 322. The fact of Faulkner's white-racist consciousness should not be used to deny the insight.

benevolent and elaborately reasoning "master." The economics of the tale, the dominant consciousness to which the author conjoins us, the rhetorical and formal structure of the story—even the style, which reflects a benevolent rationalist sensibility—insist that the character of Captain Delano be the controlling concern. Some critics ignore the disciplining requirements of the art and take the sacrificial figure, or the incompletely personified evil of the slavery situation, or quite secondary patterns of metaphor and allusion, as the essence of Melville's art and attitude. Instead, following the directions of the form, we should put considerable emphasis upon the ambiguous roles of benevolent rationalism.

Benito Cereno, unlike the other novellas, clearly derives from a written source, an historical Captain Amasa Delano's *A Narrative of Voyages and Travels.*[18] Comparison with the source confirms that Melville insufficiently digested some of his materials, particularly the excerpted legal documents of the last section of the *Narrative* which come out in Melville's story as a rather mechanical device for dramatic irony. But, as with most source comparisons, this only confirms what should be otherwise evident. The original Captain Delano appears in his own narrative as a plain and practical Yankee merchant master, remarkably confident and courageous, much concerned about the right ordering of money matters, and righteously angry about the ingratitude of duplicitous foreigners. With touches of self-pity, he presents a direct accounting of his bizarre adventures with the Spanish slave ship and its dishonest Captain. Melville's adaption eliminates the money matters and turns the crassly ungrateful and cheating Spaniard of the original into the enigmatic and sensitive Don Benito. The ships' names and some other details take on a more allegorical cast. But most important, Melville transforms the simple American's character into a rather awesome and ironical representation of a whole mode of sensibility.

[18]The source, first discovered by Harold C. Scudder and reprinted in *PMLA,* XLIV (June 1928), pp. 503-529, has often been discussed and so I only summarize a few points here.

The American's ship is renamed *Bachelor's Delight*. This fits into a personal preoccupation of Melville's—a private joke, as it were—rather than the portentous pattern of symbolism suggested by some critics. Melville, not very happily married, seems somewhat enviously and resentfully interested in defining the special qualities of bachelordom. In a sketch written a year before *Benito Cereno*, "The Paradise of Bachelors," Melville draws a favorite moral: "The thing called pain, the bugbear styled trouble—these two legends seem preposterous to . . . bachelor imaginations."[19] That remark fits oddly with Melville's drastic inability to present any substantial world of domesticity in his fictions and his glorification of the purely masculine sailor's world (even half a century away from it, as in *Billy Budd*). We should also note his grossly sentimental, and therefore probably hostile, comments in his stories on women and marriage. This hostile-sentimental masculinity fits in with his peculiarly American insistence on a "he-man" fraternity of stoic males separated from the ameliorating and complicating rest of humankind. The significance, especially for the American experience, seems to be less covert homoeroticism than the domination by compulsive laboring, to serve our exaggerated productivity, and the communion of male ritualism, to compensate for our lack of community.

In such stories as *Benito Cereno* Melville, with his rather grim view of familial order and feeling, insists upon the carefree and autonomous and benign aspect of those out of the marital morass.[20] Melville, of course, is looking back on his sailor days. Thus the bachelor Captain of the *Bachelor's Delight* appears not only endlessly genial and fraternal but the proper figure to

19"The Paradise of Bachelors," *Complete Stories*, p. 193. For the ff., contrast Fiedler, *op cit.*

20Other examples of Melville's allegorical use of bachelordom are cited by Merlin Bowen, *The Long Encounter, Self and Experience in the Writings of Herman Melville* (Chicago, 1960), pp. 66-68. He also aptly notes some similarities of failure of understanding in Vere and Delano (p. 232), but does not see this as part of Melville's pervasive critique of benevolent rationalism.

display the logic of "undistrustful good nature" and the consequences of failing to understand "malign evil in man."

Some readers, enthusiastic over the literary discovery of evil in our wicked twentieth-century world, conclude that the pleasant Yankee captain must be seen as intolerably foolish, unimaginative, insensitive, stupid, and gross for not recognizing the malign and the clever conspiracy of the blacks aboard the *San Dominick*.[21] Melville's tone, however, displays rather more subtlety than such a view allows. We must also guard against an unwarranted heroizing of Benito Cereno. The Spanish captain, sensitive and pious, provides only a partial foil to the American in the story. Cereno, understandably obsessed with the vengeance of which he has been a victim, must be evaluated as generally weak, inadequate, brooding, trapped in a Christian vision of evil that can only lead to a guilty renunciation of life. True, we can view the story as in part explaining renunciation, so difficult for optimistic Americans to accept, but that renunciation displays considerable ambiguities.[22]

Put another way, if Melville's views of the two captains were as black and white as his treatment of the slavery issue, the story would merit but little attention. The more uncertain tone suggested by the often cited opening imagery of the tale, which insists upon grayness and "shadows present, foreshadowing deeper shadows to come,"[23] is indeed appropriate. Christianity,

[21]An example is Barry Phillips who calls Delano "exclusively a fool," "a blind buffoon," "something worse than just a buffoon," a "smug American, priggish, prudent, patronizing, treacherously stupid," etc. " 'The Good Captain': A Reading of *Benito Cereno*," *Texas Studies in Literature and Language*, IV (Summer 1962), p. 191. Robert Lowell, in a rather crude contemporary adaption of *Benito Cereno*, has Delano unnecessarily kill Babo as an expression of American violence and fear. "Benito Cereno" in *The Old Glory* (New York, 1965).

[22]An altogether disproportionate concern with ostensible sources and analogues may lead to seeing *Benito Cereno* as primarily a study of Christian renunciation and the entitling figure as a literary ghost of Charles V. See H. Bruce Franklin, *The Wake of the Gods, Melville's Mythology* (Stanford, Calif., 1963), pp. 136 ff.

[23]A rather different view of the significance of the gray and isolated scene is held by those who try to add a moral correctness to Melville. Thus "nature itself . . . outraged by slavery, authorizes the vengeance of the enslaved." Harry Levin, *The Power of Blackness* (New York, 1958), p. 190.

hardly ever presented without irony in Melville, furnishes much of the shadowing effects. This is done with a series of misperceived Christian metaphors and allusions. When Delano first approaches the Spanish ship it appears to him as a "monastery," quite misleadingly. The Negroes on deck suggest a "ship-load of monks" and those seen through the open ports appear as "Black Friars pacing the cloisters." Such comparisons and analogies suggest themselves to Delano even when amidst the reality of the Spanish ship. Babo, the murderous slave leader, appears to Delano as "something like a begging friar of St. Francis." Cereno suggests a "hypochondriac abbot." When the situation seems ominous, the Protestant mariner thinks of a Guy Fawkes (Catholic) plot. Captain Cereno's manner reminds Delano of the Spaniard's "imperial countryman's, Charles V, just previous to the anchorish retirement of that monarch. . . ." I do not believe that such analogies should be read as a covert religious allegory but rather as its antithesis. They help define Cereno as the ineffective Christian who ends in Lima under the care of the monk Infelez and achieves the proper Christian end of a renunciation of life, a demand for death. Other Christian comparisons, such as Delano's misinterpreting black paganism as similar to Christian ritualism, clearly serve dramatic irony. Since the point of view of most of the story is essentially that of Captain Delano, arch-Protestant American, his would-be Catholic description of things on the Spanish ship constitutes part of his characteristic misrationalization as well as Melville's ironic treatment of traditional Christianity.[24]

Note, too, that this religious analogizing by Delano shows the sensitivity and reflectiveness Melville gives his good American. In many other details the author insists upon Delano's generous and thoughtful nature. The Yankee perceives the strange condi-

[24]In a careful examination of the religious allusions, "Melville's Saints in *Benito Cereno*," a paper delivered at the Philological Association of the Pacific Coast (Nov. 30, 1968), Professor Charles Metzger wryly suggested that Melville's use of Christianity proves that slavery produces saints. In discussion with me, he agreed that Melville's use of religious materials is almost always ironic.

tions on the Spanish ship, but "surprise was lost in pity." His "curiosity" gets subordinated to "kindness." Charity repeatedly misleads him into "ascribing reasons for strange behavior." A man of "instinctive good feeling" and "good nature," Delano usually ends "drowning criticism in compassion." His virtue becomes his vice.

Though Melville warns the reader about Delano's "honest seaman's mind" and "blunt-thinking," what we specifically see turns out to be a carefully reflective mind that reviews, analyzes and weighs events on the Spanish ship, "again and again turning over" the problems. The good American, thoughtfully principled and tempered with decorum and tolerance, sensibly examines and dismisses the idea of a malign conspiracy on the *San Dominick*. Naturally enough, he suspects not the slaves but the peculiar Spanish master of the ship. Delano decides that a conspiracy would be a rational and moral improbability.[25] Correctly reasoned, but partly wrong in fact. Moral reason that unquestioningly accepts slavery and ignores the malignity it creates is not properly cast to discover the truth.

Captain Delano's genial American tolerance—"his nature was not only benign, but familiarly and humorously so"—leads him to set aside Benito Cereno's weird (captive) behavior by a kindly bigotry: "Spaniards in the main are as good folks as any in Duxbury, Massachusetts." Such a "blithe heart" and "singular guilelessness" lead to a parochial blindness. As Benito Cereno reports in his deposition to the court, "the generosity and piety of Amasa Delano were incapable of sounding . . . wickedness." Within Delano's reasonableness, piety and goodness lies his problem—virtue as inadequacy.

Consider, for example, the egotism of goodness. Delano shows repeated pique that his virtue passes unnoticed. This leads to his

[25]Richard H. Fogle rightly argues that both theme and detail require that one *not* take Delano "for a fool." *Melville's Shorter Tales* (Norman, Okla., 1960), p. 122. However, to then see the only issues in the story as "complexity" and "mystery" and "legal truth" is to say very little.

contrasting the Spanish ship with his own ship, its master's lack of efficiency with his own orderliness, its misrule with his own discipline. His irrelevant standards reenforce his failure of perception. This encourages him to dismiss the qualms he has about the *San Dominick* because of his basic feelings of self-satisfaction. And he can thus easily reduce the strange and peculiar to his own background and homey comparisons. Since he acknowledges only "benevolent thoughts" in his own mind, he does the same for the minds of others. When something seems amiss in the others, he examines his own conscience and concludes, "well satisfied," that "nothing in his own conduct could justify it," and therefore it may be ignored. On leaving the Spanish ship, irritated at the strangely ungracious behavior of its captain, he reflects on his own correctness and virtue and decides "one's conscience is never ungrateful." Good conscience serves as another name for insular egotism. Notice, too, his charming answer to himself about his suspicions that there might be a plot against him:

What, I, Amasa Delano—Jack of the Beach, as they called me when a lad—I, Amasa; the same that, duck-satchel in hand, used to paddle along the water-side to the school house made from the old hulk—I, little Jack of the Beach, that used to go berrying with cousin Nat and the rest; I to be murdered here at the ends of the earth, on board a haunted pirate ship by a horrible Spaniard? Too nonsensical to think of: Who would murder Amasa Delano? His conscience is clean, There is someone above, Fie, fie, Jack of the Beach: you are a child indeed. . . .

Indeed he is, with that self-centered "I" four times in the first sentence, that touchingly irrelevant picture of himself as all childhood innocence, and that peculiar logic in which he can't be murdered because his "conscience is clean." An egotistical religion, a moralistic Christianity, provides the final assurance. Similarly with a later episode when Delano's mind, in spite of himself, "swarmed with superstitious suspicions," but he finds solace in the irrelevantly "benign aspect of nature" and corrects his feelings in that "he should, by implication, have betrayed an atheist doubt of the ever-watchful Providence above." Such Protestant faith in the direct relation to the deity obscures rather than focuses awareness of outside evil, and probably encourages pious goodness becoming blind egotism.

However perceptive and thoughtful, the self-centeredness derived from a faith in a benevolent universe must falsify the American's intuitive sense of reality. Surely this provides much of the case pessimist Melville intends to make with his American character. The culminating point in Delano's obtuseness is also the turning point in the melodrama. The desperate Benito Cereno leaps into Delano's departing boat in order to escape his imprisonment. Delano assumes that his own person must be the intended victim of the ungrateful and vile Spanish captain. When Babo, knife in hand, pursues Cereno into the American boat, Delano still assumes that Delano is the intended victim. Only as Babo makes a second attempt to stab Cereno does Delano, with a "flash of revelation," finally comprehend his obtuseness. Never having thought of anyone else as the victim of conspiracy and danger, and never having considered the other as different from his own conscience and well-being, he has twisted what he must deep-down know—otherwise it would not all suddenly fit together. Decency, in its selfish conceit and benevolently rationalized irrelevance, can falsify awareness to the point of destruction.

Melville seems to elaborate much of the analysis of Captain Delano with special insistence on his representative American-ness. The good Yankee displays many of our more genial big-otries, still identifiable as part of our national style. At one point he explains away the inadequacy of the trapped Benito Cereno by supposing that the aristocratic Spaniard must have achieved his command by way of the "cabin-window" rather than the "hawse-hole"—he was not a self-made man. Though probably true, it serves, again, as an irrelevant self-congratulation for the self-made Yankee. The American's too easy sense of equality also allows him to patronize the Negroes while blaming the foreign aristocrat's arbitrary authority for everything that appears wrong on the Spanish ship. Although Delano is right in viewing Captain Cereno as unmanly—his scabbard is empty—the American should have recognized that authority without power must mean that someone else—Babo—had the real power.[26] But it gratifies the good American too much to explain away the conditions on the Spanish ship as its Captain's failings in self-indulgence, morbidity, over-refinement, arrogance, supercilious heritage, splenetic superiority, and general decadence. Such, to a Melville skeptical of the democratic credo in a malignant world, become the fallacies of vulgar "democratic" prejudices and arrogant Americanism. Melville, as it were, makes an *ad hominem* argument to mock our usual *ad hominem* arguments.

In assuming that "distress" must result from practical and moral incompetence, this Protestant American applies to the Old World what Americans now often apply to their own poor and dissident. For Delano, Cereno's troubles must result from "faulty" command and "incompetence" in genial mastery. As we can see so often in American history, this credo becomes righteous when we insist, like Delano, on linking "pain and abashment . . . with vice." Then the victims must be blamed.

We still publicly hold that healthy efficiency and genial virtue resolve most human difficulties. Such reductive moralizing must distort complex reality and force elaborate rationalization. When, under pressure from Babo, Cereno questions Captain Delano about the size of his crew and the number of his weapons, Delano rightly fears for a moment. But, with his powers of prac-

---

[26]Note the trite conservative moral drawn by Nicholas Canaday, Jr.: *Benito Cereno* "reveals the disorder attendant upon authority without power and the barbarity of power without authority." *Melville and Authority* (Gainesville, Fla., 1968), p. 22. He fails to note that Cereno's authority as slave master, like that of the Lima court, is also "barbaric." Indeed, a better rule would be that legitimized power is usually more efficiently vicious than non-legitimatized, and that real authority—the genuine ability to lead, to know, to say, to do—is usually better when it does not have direct and formal power.

tical analysis, he dismisses the questioning as too obviously done, and thus not to be taken as threatening. "Thus, the same conduct which had raised the alarm, served to dispel it." Here Melville makes a favorite philosophical point: the double-edged and inadequate nature of reason itself. Rationality serves the will, the purposes and the world-view, of the reasoner. Delano's reasoning can be no more adequate than his view of life and himself. Reason exists no more independently than goodness. Rationality trails rather than creates our view of life.

Curiously, Melville sensitizes the character of his good American. No Babbitt he. Instead of being rough, as we initially expect, the Captain displays a delicate tolerance. In never harshly breaking through the forced restraints of Benito Cereno, in never demanding answers of him or being overtly critical, Delano avoids finding out the truth. Genial tolerance maintains the masquerade, continues what is. Full of justified "trepidations," Delano exerted "his good nature to the utmost" and "insensibly he came to a compromise" explanation that explained nothing. When he sees Babo use the Spanish flag as a barber's sheet on the terrified Cereno—the shaving by the rebel slave leader is a diabolical scene—Delano good-humoredly passes off the startling effrontery. In this shaving scene, the American twice senses a reality contrary to the conspiratorial masquerade, yet dismisses such thoughts as "antic conceits." In another scene, he "began to quake at thoughts he barely durst confess to himself" but, again, laughs them away as "hobgoblins." Only in such hobgoblins and antic awareness could he have discovered the anguished human reality.

Melville employs a number of allegorical devices to reenforce his description of the awareness the American needs.[27] An intricate knot provides one. Entangled in his uncertainties about the Spanish ship, Captain Delano focuses on an elaborate knot a

[27]Some of the devices, but oddly not some of those discussed here, are related together by Guy Cardwell, "Melville's Gray Story: Symbols and Meaning in *Benito Cereno*," *Bucknell Review*, VIII (May 1959), pp. 163 ff.

sailor is working. After a bit of enigmatic warning, the sailor throws the knot (apparently containing a message) to Delano with instructions to "undo it, cut it, quick." But the American, no man for dealing with eccentric tangles and "gordian" complexities, "unconsciously" hands the knot over to a suspicious black guard. Puzzled, interested, perplexed, squeamish—"knot in hand, knot in head"—he naturally rejects all knotted thought and feeling. Thus the Spanish Captain appears to the American as alternately "wicked imposture" and "innocent lunacy," but not as knotted in a much more perplexing possibility. That the good American obscurely fears and avoids as deeply threatening to his basic view of life.

Melville's propensity for the knotted analogy, for the artful and over-artful moralizing, regularly threatens in his writings to become the dominant substance. An extremely limited dramatist—his characters rarely reveal significant unfolding or transformation—the illustration becomes the art. Even his melodramatic action seems to take place in a static, unameliorable world, in which riddling interpretation becomes the main concern. In *Benito Cereno* he uses a whole series of allegorical devices: the "flawed bell" of the *San Dominick* in which the normal marks of time reverberate with strange resonances (this *is* a different order); the railing of the quarter deck that rottenly breaks after Delano engages in romantic reveries (that exclusive area of maritime authority is disintegrating); the strange sensations and intimations the American frighteningly finds (and eagerly loses) in dark places on the foreign ship; and the emblematic and quaint and deathly devices surrounding him and which, like the pitch that defiles an innocent sailor's hand, he moralistically rationalizes away. Even those final documents, those depositions of Benito Cereno and others for the court, raise an appropriate perplexity as well as provide ironic information.[28] They will serve,

28Newton Arvin objected strongly to the aesthetic effect of the legal documents, and followed through by denying all other significance to the story. *Herman Melville* (New York, 1950), pp. 238 ff. Some of the least interesting readings see the

says the author, "as the key to fit the lock of the complications." In fact, they do not. We have seen, with the lock-and-key image about the royal black, how misleading such keys can be. The documents, restricted as is almost always true with legal materials to the narrow purposes of the court, tell us little about Babo and the crucial slavery background, and not at all enough about Benito Cereno. The "deep-diving" of the story—to use Melville's point from *Moby Dick*—suggests the inadequacy of all explanations, all strange knottings, and that the full dark truth remains in doubt.

One question, however, is carefully answered by the story. The author early asked whether or not such a "benevolent heart" as that of his American went along with sufficient "intellectual perception" of "what humanity is capable" of being. That, says the narrator, "may be left to the wise to determine." Given the wisdom gained from the story, the determination seems rather certain: the representative good American and benevolent rationalist reveals a quite inadequate perception of the dark human realities. Yet we must, following Melville's treatment of the materials, remain in some perplexity. Captain Cereno was not wrong, the ending confirms, in judging from the start that the Spanish Captain was "prey to settled dejection" or, as he later puts it, "one whose spirit has been crushed by misery." Delano, of course, cannot see the profundity of that misery which points beyond the immediate situation to the evil condition of life itself: death. Yet the benevolent rationalist not only saved his own life, and that of his crew, but, short of final despair, that of Benito Cereno and some of the Spanish sailors. Melville's irony once again cuts both ways; the good American, *because* of his limitations, has been good and achieved good. We remain, then, as apparently did Melville, with an ambivalent view of the good but terribly limited American.

---

story simply as a puzzle with the law finally answering all questions. See, for example, James E. Miller, Jr., *A Reader's Guide to Melville* (New York, 1962), p. 153.

The bones of slave-master Aranda, above Babo's savage adjuration of "Follow your leader," guide the ship and its ostensible master to bitter darkness. This image of vengeful death "substituted for the ship's proper figure head" of Christopher Columbus also mocks the brutal realities of the New World. Note, too, how Melville plays upon the point: the American mate, in boarding the Spanish slave ship in battle with the blacks, repeats the warning, "Follow your leader," and repeats the brutality. The American belief in the bright sun and gentle winds, in the positive and practical and providential, instead of the shadows and black forces of perplexity and malignancy and death, should not be easily dismissed. But how will the American virtues serve when death is the figurehead of our voyage? The Delano-virtues of geniality, compromise, practicality and faith will not do for the deep and dark truths of the human condition. They cannot provide authentic choices in confronting annihilation. We might wish that our traditional good Americans were not passé but we must also recognize that our benevolent rationalists lack that most basic "intellectual perception" of what life is about.

4. *The Despair of Logic*

In Leo Tolstoy's brilliant study of the ordinary middle class man as benevolent rationalist. *The Death of Ivan Ilyich,* the desperately ill and despairing official reflects:

The syllogism he had learned from Kiezewetter's Logic: "Caius is a man, men are mortal, therefore Caius is mortal," had always seemed to him correct as applied to Caius, but certainly not as applied to himself. That Caius—man in the abstract—was mortal, was perfectly correct, but he was not Caius, not an abstract man, but a creature quite, quite separate. . . . "It cannot be that I ought to die. That would be too terrible."[29]

[29]*The Short Novels of Tolstoy* (Maude translation), ed. Philip Rahv (New York, 1946), pp. 445-446.

Rather more incisively than ponderous Heidegger, and more harshly than ambiguous Melville, Tolstoy sets logic aside from the realization of the truth about the fundamentals of existence. As part of his passionate despair, of course, Tolstoy also attempts to reverse the annihilating dread of death with Ivan's final radicalization and death-bed moment of illumination into love. Yet, in his oblique way, Melville pushes further. Not only does he elaborate the misleading nature of reason and a benignly providential view of life, he allows no redemption. Cereno despairs unto death; Delano remains essentially unchanged even after the revelatory experience; and the ill-used, however malignant, Babo becomes the black mocking death-head that oversees all. Melville, again, ends in nihilism, and a despair of any logic of hope.

Once one breaks through the artifices of traditional piety and autonomous rationality, the nuclear experiences become decisive. For those of impassioned skepticism, the dark human reality must reveal itself as the nothingness of death. Malignity and masquerade in *Benito Cereno*, like the judicial murder and myth in *Billy Budd*, simply provide mocking variations on the loss of faith and the power of death. Falsity and fear and evil and despair derive their meaning from mortality; the rest, for Melville, turns out to be masquerade and myth. Because he relates all human logic to the processes of such annihilation, Melville stands as the most metaphysical of writers. This abstract insistence and nihilistic sense does not often encourage Melville towards the possibilities of more humane concern, nor to any logic beyond that of dread, though some there may be.

Comparing the pattern of *Benito Cereno* to those of *Billy Budd* and *Bartleby*, we see the similarities of Melville's dialectics in the three stories. Perhaps the most striking difference in *Benito Cereno* appears in the division or doubling of the victim. For in spite of Melville's efforts, we can hardly accept Babo as the pure dark diabolism of Claggart; he takes on some of the sacrificial significance of a Billy Budd and a Bartleby.[30] The passivity, the saintly overtones, the pathos, go to Benito Cereno. It seems evident that Melville cast his figures so that Babo is to Claggart as Delano is to Vere and Benito Cereno to Billy Budd. Yet Babo carries a defiant heroism as well as providing the penultimate death-head image of the parable. Our sympathy with the revolting black slave, rather greater than Melville's, gives some ambiguity to *Benito Cereno*. The poetry of Melville's meditation on death seems to conflict with the melodramatic form. That the good American lives on, as the melodrama requires, gives additional ambiguity, appropriate also to Melville's feelings about the American character. That Captain Delano, less vicious than Captain Vere though no less prone to legal murder,[31] survives seems more ironic than any adequacy of benevolent rationalism. For Melville's dominant subject is false consciousness, put not in ameliorating but annihilating perspective, as the style and concern of the whole story insist.

Should we wish further morals for *Benito Cereno* than the shattering of false consciousness—including the futility of Christian resignation, the black-white malignancy of Manichean dualism, and the obtuseness of benevolent rationalism—we should have to find a logic that goes beyond despair. But there would be some difficulty in attributing it to Melville. Any relevant hope, he seems to insist, would have to first admit darkness into the light, a full and everyday absorption of death into con-

---

[30]I believe that in effect I am answering the suggestion that the "real problem" of *Benito Cereno* is "in discovering the implications of the masquerade." Edgar A. Dryden, *Melville's Thematics of Form* (Baltimore, Md., 1968), p. 202. Myth and masquerade tend to be equivalent for skeptical Melville, and focus similar Pyrrhic irony.

[31]A few discussions of Vere in *Billy Budd* note the resemblance to Delano in *Benito Cereno*. See, for example, Ralph W. Willett, "Nelson and Vere: Hero and Victim in *Billy Budd, Sailor*," *PMLA*, LXXXII (October 1967), pp. 370-376. He implies that such second-rate figures of authority are bound to be ambiguous. Delano's Americanism, of course, makes him a considerably more genial figure, similar in this respect to Bartleby's attorney, and therefore the viciousness is less emphatic than it is with Vere.

sciousness. There cannot be accurate perception, much less wis dom, without the intense sense of mortality. Without that existential condition, choices and life-styles will be false. Probably in most ordinary senses we should have to achieve a shape of things beyond mere logic. Certainly we would have to break out of what Heidegger calls "the impersonal mode of social existence"; or what Tolstoy describes as the thingification of one's self as acceptable magistrate, concerned owner, proper husband, clinical problem, compulsive card-player, or other depersonalization; or out of what Melville dramatizes as the obtusely benign and rationalizing good American. All constitute the false objectification of human existence, the destructive division of the total responsive self.

Perhaps the nineteenth-century sensibilities of Melville and Tolstoy and Heidegger obscure the need for the transformation of consciousness to be a fully biological and social holism, a polymorphous unity of body and mind and world which incorporates death into passionate life.[32] The alternative, as Melville's bitter imagination perceived, provides only the stripped bones on the prow, vengeance, renunciation and false consciousness. That leaves us echoing, as do the assaulting Americans, the bitter revolting slave's admonition above the stripped bones, "Follow your leader," and being mastered by a mocking black death-head.

---

[32]For a statement of part of the issue here, see Kingsley Widmer, "The Prophecies of Passion," *Centennial Review*, XI (Winter 1967), pp. 82-101.

CHAPTER FOUR

BARTLEBY AND
NIHILISTIC RESISTANCE

1. *The Perverse Clerk*

Some of the significance of Melville's *Bartleby*, "The Scrivener, A Story of Wall Street,"[1] in several senses a unique work in spite of many parallels with the other short novels, might be suggested by a monologue Melville implied but did not write. For the entitling figure of the story remains, like rebel slave Babo, wilfully silent, or almost so. A copy clerk in a New York law office, Bartleby mysteriously declines to do his work or even to explain why he refuses. As he tells his employer, a decent and reasonable attorney, "I prefer not to be a little reasonable." Finally, he prefers to accusingly haunt the office until hauled off to prison, where he ends by preferring not even to live. As in the other short novels, Melville focuses primarily on the benevolently rationalizing figure of authority; to him, as to the reader, the perverse clerk must remain enigmatic, a moral and intellectual perplexity. But since some readers insist on discussing the character Bartleby, in spite of the narrator's warning in the

[1] All references to *Bartleby* are to the printing in *The Complete Stories of Herman Melville*, ed. Jay Leyda (New York, 1949), pp. 3-47. Because of the many brief quotations, individual page references are not given. I know of no significant textual problems. The periodical version of the story appears in facsimile in *Bartleby the Scrivener*, "Melville Annual," ed. Howard P. Vincent (Kent, Ohio, 1966). This includes a good bibliography through 1964 by Donald A. Fiene, pp. 140-148, though the ff. annotations are sometimes rather misleading. The two interesting articles included with the academic chaff in this volume will be cited later.

first paragraph ("Bartleby was one of those beings of whom nothing was ascertainable. . . ."), it may be useful to give part of the Bartleby rationale, the prefer-not-to dialectic of wise perversity and modern intellectual anti-rationalism:

Oh, tell me, who first declared, who first proclaimed, that man only does nasty things because he does not know his own real interests; and that if he were enlightened, if his eyes were opened to his real normal interests, man would at once cease to do nasty things, would at once become good and noble because, being enlightened and understanding his real advantage, he would see his own advantage in the good and nothing else, and we all know that not a single man can knowingly act to his own disadvantage. . . . [But] what is to be done with the millions of facts that bear witness that men, *knowingly*, that is, fully understanding their real advantages, have left them in the background and have rushed headlong on another path, to risk, to chance, compelled to this course by nobody and and by nothing, but, as it were, precisely because they did not want the beaten path, and stubbornly, wilfully, went off on another difficult, absurd way seeking it almost in the darkness. After all, it means that this stubbornness and willfulness were more pleasant to them than any advantage. Advantage! What is advantage? And will you take it upon yourself to define with perfect accuracy in exactly what the advantage of man consists? . . . it seems that something that is dearer to almost every man than his greatest advantages must really exist, or (not to be illogical) there is one most advantageous advantage . . . which is more important and more advantageous than all other advantages, for which, if necessary, a man is ready to act in opposition to all laws, that is, in opposition to reason, honor, peace, prosperity—in short, in opposition to all those wonderful and useful things if only he can attain that fundamental, most advantageous advantage which is dearer to him than all.

". . . let us live once more according to our foolish will!" . . . man everywhere and always, whoever he may be, has preferred to act as he wishes and not in the least as his reason and advantage dictated.

Why, one may choose what is contrary to one's own interests, and sometimes one *positively ought*. . . . One's own free unfettered choice, one's own fancy, however wild it may be, one's own fancy worked up at times to frenzy—why that is that very "most advantageous advantage" which we have overlooked, which comes under no classification and through which all systems and theories are continually being sent to the devil. And how do these sages know that man must necessarily need a rationally advantageous choice? What man needs is simply *independent* choice, whatever that independence may cost and wherever it may lead.

. . . reason, gentlemen, is an excellent thing, there is no disputing that, but reason is only reason and can only satisfy man's rational faculty, while will is a manifestation of all life. . . . I insist on my caprice. . . .[2]

Though this philosophical monologue is that of another capricious clerk in another nineteenth century novella—Dostoyevsky's "anti-hero" in *Notes from the Underground*—it could just as well be that of Melville's Bartleby if he were to reveal himself in a frenziedly paradoxical self-argument. Both clerks, appropriate genteel-bitter personifications of the human toll taken by the dominant nineteenth century ideology, make desperate assertions of their residual humanity. Some of the perplexity around these figures comes from the archness of their authors, so aware of the loss of values and defending a desperate stoicism (Melville) and an equally desperate Christianity (Dostoyevsky). And some of the perplexity comes from the essential ambiguity of characters at once pathetically sick and astutely wise. The double view inherent in such compounding quite properly disturbs the reader. As with the twentieth century American Dostoyevskyean novella, *Miss Lonelyhearts* (in which the homosexual newspaper reporter with disabling obsessional behavior is also the visionary

2My quotation links together several passages from the monologue of Part I, *Notes from the Underground*, ed. and trans. Ralph E. Matlaw (New York, 1960), pp. 18-27.

modern Christ who martyrs himself to the reality of suffering) the combination of the pathological and profound violates our expectations.[3] Symptoms become insights and insightfullness becomes an illness. No doubt the greater danger in discussing such figures would be to reduce them to clinical proportions, as often happens. Their undeniable pathology provides as well as conditions their perceptions, and ours. We cannot ignore that the brilliant psychopaths who serve as the existential spokesmen of modernist sensibility also act out human distortions and a pervasive nihilism. But those seem to be the minimum requirements of our tragic human awareness.

The perverse clerk's very existence constitutes an affront to the dominant metapsychology of Western civilization, at least since the eighteenth century, and the assumption that we understand and control all men by "self-interest" (Dostoyevsky's "advantage"). Marxism as well as "classical" political-economic theory, utilitarian ethics as well as applied Christian morality, largely depend on the appeal to an organizable form of selfishness. The outrageousness of a man-from-the-underground or a Bartleby systematically denying all such appeals, and with absurd arrogance and the wisdom of failure refusing the motivations and resisting the ethics of self-interest, puts the grim cast of repression on all of our ostensibly rational order. Our psychological and moral tactics lose their benevolent appearance and reveal a tyrannical warping of the human and a destruction of freedom. How dare these miserable clerks! They insist on the primacy of preference and will, these wan and lonely creatures in their subterranean and impotent lives which end in perversity and self-destruction. A sardonic pathos qualifies their exalted claims to individuality and freedom. Only imaginations at once sternly

[3]See Kingsley Widmer, "The Sweet and Savage Prophecies of Nathaneal West," *The Thirties,* ed. Warren French (Deland, Fla., 1968). In both discussions I draw upon an unpublished discussion of Dostoyevsky. Melville, we should note, also identified with sickness-is-wisdom tradition of dark art, writing in *Moby Dick,* for example, that "all mortal greatness is but disease."

conservative and radically nihilistic could generate such exacerbated tropes. They pay for their awareness with despair, and their apocalyptic vision furthers a radical resistance to them as well as to our world.

2. The Perplexed Critics

Because *Bartleby* appears to be a considerable departure, in manner as in subject, from Melville's earlier and later sea stories, and because of its more clearly evident nihilism, many readers find this work especially puzzling. Therefore much of the learned criticism seeks to remake the enigmatic fable. Scholarly criticism sometimes serves institutional culture by trying to adapt the peculiarities of the modern imagination to more acceptable ideologies. In its more competent efforts, academic literary study would ameliorate the extremities of modernist art and reduce them to the very benevolent rationalism under attack by that art. To avoid this with *Bartleby* we must accept the enigma of the entitling figure and, without bland reduction, follow Melville's mocking dialectics of negation. Certainly part of the charm of the tale comes from its extremity, its refusal of any reasonable resolution and its fusion of outrageous comedy and bitter pathos. This "absurdist" tone confirms the logic of refusal.[4]

Who and what is the perverse clerk who prefers not to do everything and anything, including living? Though commonly asked, that seems to be the wrong question. With most authors, especially in the earlier history of fiction, we find at least an implicit logic by which we may assume a past and pattern for the characters. But here Melville seems to carefully undercut such constructs. Exasperated readers may be tempted to give too solid flesh to the reverberating gestures and metaphysical metaphors with which Melville both defines and confines the figure

---

[4]Many post-World War II critics cite, as I did in my earlier study of *Bartleby*, similarities to Franz Kafka's stories. While relevant to the genre, and twentieth century ("modernist") tone, the comparisons may be misleading in other ways.

of Bartleby—"mystery," "solitude," "forlorn," "preference," "will," "perverseness," "melancholy," and similar repeated abstract tropes. These must be taken as the fundamentals of Bartleby's existence. Only at issue is our way of responding to them. Similarly, Bartleby must be accepted in his many times repeated sad and delightful "I prefer not to." This disconcerting mixture of politeness and defiance, this summary phrase of a radically passive resistance, provides both the essence of the figure and the major resonant moral of the tale. We should refrain from undercutting it.

Before considering Melville's analysis of representative rational, and American, response to this wry rebellion, we might briefly consider some scholarly examples. Confronted with the enigmatic and ambiguous, some look for a "key" to secret purpose and meaning. Could *Bartleby* be such a perplexity because the author covertly wrote about someone he knew? Melville did have an uncle attorney and several brothers with offices in the Wall Street district. He also had a friend who worked in a law office and ended in a mental hospital.[5] Such sources certainly could have provided satiric and pathetic material for the story. But we should not confuse sources with the art, the material with the meaning. And none of the recognizable source material suggests the peculiarities of Bartleby, or the dialectics of the narrator's elaborate self-arguments about his defiant scrivener. Also, the story seems far less concerned with Wall Street actualities—the atmosphere is isolated from the real world, the treatment is fantastic, and the tone is quietly grotesque—than with

[5]Jay Leyda points out possible source figures in Melville's uncle-lawyer and in Melville's two brothers with law offices on Wall Street. He also suggests a source for Bartleby in a friend of Melville's, Eli Fly, who worked in a law office and ended up in a mental hospital. "Notes on Sources," *The Complete Stories*, p. 455. Melville's father-in-law was also a lawyer-judge who may have had something to say about his son-in-law's limited success in making money as a writer. Leon Howard connects Bartleby with Melville's friend George F. Adler, who was confined in a mental hospital in 1853. *Herman Melville* (Los Angeles, Calif., 1951), p. 208. The equation of Bartleby with mental hospital patients is the peculiarity of Melville scholars since there is no suggestion of it in the story.

recurrent intellectual preoccupations we find in other writings of Melville's.

Could Melville have been doing a satiric though abstracted sketch of some famous contemporary? Several have been suggested, most notably Henry David Thoreau.[6] Bartleby's corner of the office is several times called a "hermitage," its occupant seems to be a vegetarian, and, most important, he practices a form of passive resistance analogous to Thoreau's famed civil disobedience. But no other important similarity seems evident, and the scene and manner certainly do not correspond with such a source. The comparison of Bartleby and the hero-author of *Walden* and *Civil Disobedience* produces only a mildly interesting association of ideas and does not explicate or elaborate much of the story.

More far fetched analogies, partly dependent on scholarly knowledge of Melville's reading, have been suggested. Bartleby gets variously described as a Christian martyr or a Buddhistic contemplative[7] or a Hindu saint.[8] Oddly, the most appropriate such free association seems to have not yet been publicly made— Bartleby as Taoist holy man.[9] Of course almost *any* parabolic literary figure can suggest *some* similarities with some part or other of the great religious myths and symbologies. That, essentially, is their function. The main utility these days of traditional

[6]Apparently the first equation of Bartleby and Thoreau was by Egbert S. Oliver, "A Second Look at 'Bartleby'," *College English*, VI (May 1945), pp. 431-439.

[7]Walter Sutton made the equation of Bartleby with Buddhism, since followed by several other interpreters. "Melville and the Great God Budd," *Prairie Schooner*, XXXIV (Summer 1960), pp. 128-129.

[8]Bartleby as Hindu saint is developed in terms of loose parallels with Oriental materials Melville may have read. See H. Bruce Franklin, *The Wake of the Gods, Melville's Mythology* (Stanford, Calif., 1963), pp. 135 ff. He also cites the Christ parallels many critics have noted and which probably would fit the majority of suffering characters in some hundreds of years of our literature.

[9]For those who wish to elaborate the Taoist analogy, I suggest two rather different views of the Taoist holy man: Max Kaltenmark, *Lao Tzu and Taoism* (Stanford, Calif., 1969); and Holmes Welch's most interesting *Taoism: The Parting of the Way* (Boston, 1966).

mythological erudition would seem to be providing racks on which to hang diverse aesthetic experiences in a world in which they no longer naturally hang together. In contrast, our own real myths—from scientism and technology, from the fetishism of consumer culture, and from our socio-political ideologies—take us over in far less self-conscious and synthetic ways than the quaint patterns of traditional mythologies. The classical mythic comparisons depend rather more on their ingenious use by learned readers than by Melville. Though the analogizing may be a pleasant scholarly game, the drawing of such parallels obscures more than it tells. The re-mythicizers say little about the argument and attitude embodied in the work because they build a substitute system. Their equivalents neither explicate nor explain, and tend to cover up the original dialectic of the literature.

Certainly the parallels with Bartleby need not be, and have not been, confined to the obvious world religions. Melville's prose reflects not only bits of Oriental mythology but also the burlesque humor of Thomas Carlyle and Charles Dickens.[10] Some readers see the allegorical manner of *Bartleby* linking with the tales of Hawthorne and Poe, both of whom may be minor influences, given the time and place. But finding special sources for *Bartleby* seems unnecessary. The paired, father-son, figures of sacrificial victim and rationalizing authority, the melancholy isolation and mutedly heroic failure, the obsessive concern with freedom and will, defiance and law, and much else—from parallel titles to Pyrrhic endings—show close similarities to other novellas of the author's. These parallels deserve more emphasis than they usually receive. Besides, the figure of Bartleby might more profitably be used as itself a basic analogue rather than as derivative of other analogues. He, and his "I prefer not to," originate an archetypal figure on which to base comparisons—and one more pertinent to us than a good many standard saints—the ulti-

[10]Several of these are cited below.

mate passive resister who sacrificially defies the conventional limits and barriers to the annihilating awareness of life. We may reserve a high-lighted corner for Bartleby—near the Good Soldier Schweik?—in the group portrait of the mythic rebels.

The most often insisted upon "key" to Bartleby does base itself on Melville but in a rather reductive autobiographical way. The logic usually goes something like this: Melville was a forlorn writer, especially since his previous ambitious works—the unique *Moby Dick* and the muddled *Pierre*—did badly in earning money and praise and understanding; the forlorn Bartleby is a scrivener, a writer (actually, law scriveners mostly copied); in sum, writer Bartleby is writer Melville and expresses the author's sense of despair in mid-nineteenth century America because it allowed little recognition or place to a serious—a critical and pessimistic—artist.[11] Some trite political ideologists add, just because of the subtitle, "A Story of Wall Street," that *Bartleby* must also be an attack on American capitalism's mistreatment of writers.[12]

[11]Apparently the first systematic equation of Melville and Bartleby, so often repeated, was made by Lewis Mumford, *Herman Melville* (New York, 1929, 1962), pp. 162 ff. This shows the remarkable staying power of an early biographical speculation. My summary is a composite of a number of such interpretations. Evidence of how standard the scrivener Melville equation has become is indicated by popular introductions. See, for example, *Eight Great American Short American Novels*, ed. Philip Rahv (New York, 1963), pp. 10-11.

[12]The most arbitrary of the biographical allegorizings is that of Leo Marx. He describes the narrating attorney as the "boss" in the headquarters of American capitalism where most writers (the two minor comic scriveners) are submissive "wage earners." Melville, then, attacks "the sacred right of private property" and makes an "unequivocal case against Wall Street society for its treatment of the writer." Somehow, too, Bartleby's nihilism expresses "hope" for the "average man" because of Melville's self-directed "rebuke to the self-absorbtion of the artist." Marx also makes this curious interpretation depend on far-fetched symbolic interpretations of colors and other details based on bits from writings of other periods, then concludes that this proves the failure of the art since it is "a grave defect of the parable that we must go back" to the earlier works. "Melville's Parable of the Walls," *Sewanee Review*, LXI (Autumn 1953), pp. 602-627. I quote this not only to illustrate several kinds of bad criticism but also because the piece has become a standard citation in Melville scholarship, probably for irrelevant reasons.

Though the American treatment of intellectuals and artists often, and perhaps usually, unjustly and extravagantly rewards those who suit the purposes of markets and institutions and cliques, *Bartleby* does not provide much of a case against Wall Street capitalists and American commercialism and our fraudulent literary life. Besides, Melville did rather well in becoming, for a time, a best-seller with his adventure books, *Typee* and *Omoo*, in having suitable connections to publish in popular magazines, and in getting a number of eccentric works, such as *Moby Dick*, published. On the whole, Melville was, in the crass senses, lucky and well rewarded. That he was not sufficiently manipulative and conventional to be a permanent literary success is rather beside the point.

As to Bartleby, there seems to be no logic directly relating him to the problems of commercialism. Money, the narrator repeatedly notes, provides no issue for his scrivener. Melville's Wall Street does not serve its later propagandistic function as an image of financial power and control, something only fully developed with late-nineteenth century Populism. Primarily, Melville's Wall Street serves as a metaphysical metaphor of confinement and barriers to understanding. Certainly the plight of lonely and drudging clerks can be said to inform the story, but they, unfortunately, are not peculiar to capitalism and America. If one wishes to relate the story more broadly to "the spirit of capitalism," of the Protestant ethic and a narrow pragmatic rationality and a sensibility of prudent self-interest, that might well be more appropriate. But as a more direct socio-economic plaint or indictment, the story can only seem an obtuse and irrelevant allegory. That, of course, may be the fault of those who insist, on most dubious grounds, on reading it that way.

What about the projective equation of Melville with forlorn "writer" Bartleby? A writer's fantasy projection more usually reveals itself in discrepancy than in similarity—the impotent clerk-type who imagines himself a lusty adventurer or the involuted introspective who projects himself as a decisive political leader. While not everything in literature need be viewed as compensatory, that process would be more likely than one producing reductive self-images. Our literature is full of reversed images of the authors, from our nineteenth century sick puritans dramatizing figures of passion to a court jester like Norman Mailer dreaming himself a charismatic politician. The psychological equation of Melville and Bartleby seems unusually thin; more interesting would be the equation of Melville with the figures of ambivalent authority, such as Captains Vere and Delano and Bartleby's attorney. But hardly any of the critics explore this suggestive possibility for the discontented Melville.

The most widely practiced biographical game with *Bartleby* comes down heavily on a rather literal pun with "dead letters." After Bartleby's death, the narrating attorney says he acquired a "vague report" that was never verified suggesting that his scrivener had previously worked in the "Dead Letter Office." As we shall see in examining the narrator, this sort of rationalizing of a present issue by way of a reductive cause quite fits the attorney and the argument Melville makes against him. But even if we force this rumor to serve as a fact really explaining Bartleby, and then rather arbitrarily ask how it can be applied to Melville, the emphasis of the self-pity may still point elsewhere.[13] For we are told that Bartleby lost his job in the Dead Letter Office due to "a change in the administration." Melville, of course, was writing in the pre-civil service days of political patronage. In the early 1850s his relatives, including his attorney father-in-law, tried to get Herman Melville a political appointment, a consulship such as Hawthorne had, and in the 1860s finally succeeded in getting Melville an appointment as an Inspector of Customs in New York. Here, if we insist on one, may be the practical

---

[13]Harry Levin, following the stock equation of Bartleby and Melville, sees the scrivener not as the attorney's "double" but as Melville's and thus presenting his "retreat from the profession of letters." *The Power of Blackness* (New York, 1958), pp. 187-188. One difficulty with this interpretation is that Melville went on to write half a dozen more books.

autobiographical connection between author and character. Its lack of portentous interest to the modern reader would not make the allusion less pertinent to the author. If we wish a more subtle psychological symbolization, I suggest that we might view Bartleby as expressing a deeper failure of Melville as man, not as artist, and consider the forlornness resulting from his sense of marital defeat or the guilt from his ambivalent submission and rebellion towards authority.[14]

Yet most of the scholars only play upon the pun of "dead letters" as Melville's writings, with the usual solipsism of modern literary scholarship. "Conceive," says the narrator, "a man by nature and misfortune prone to a pallid hopelessness, can any business seem more fitted to heighten it than that of continually handling these dead letters, and assorting them for the flames?" Some of the quasi-biographers refer to a fire at Melville's publisher, which apparently happened after *Bartleby* was written.[15] The narrator of *Bartleby* cites several maudlin examples of "dead letters" and then adds, "On errands of life, these letters speed to death." Possibly this passage could be covertly intensified by Melville's feelings about his writings and a sense of them as dead letters to humanity, but success as a writer probably had little to do with such feelings. A serious pessimist, such as Melville surely was, can hardly be assuaged for the futility of his words by the multiplication of dubious readers. That would simply increase the messages on the way to death. Rather obviously, *Bartleby* develops at length themes larger than literary careerism, including the more fundamental failure of human

[14]Henry A. Murray, though continuing the Melville-Bartleby stock equation, at least relates some motifs in the novella to Melville's marital despair. "Bartleby and I," *Bartleby*, ed. Vincent, pp. 3-24.

[15]I first heard the equation of the burning of the "dead letters" and the burning of Melville's manuscripts in a fire at Harper's in a lecture by Alfred Kazin (1950). He insisted that this biographical parallelism and the attack on a capitalistic Wall Street were the only possible meanings of the story. Other critics repeat both points. However, the fire apparently took place December 10, 1853, while the story, published in the November and December editions of *Putnam's*, must have been written before the fire.

communication, properly reinforced by the metaphor of dead letters.[16] Whatever personal sense of guilt and defeat Melville drew upon, here he seems to again lament not so much himself as the larger isolation of man and the frequent futility of his endeavours.[17]

Such larger philosophic concerns would be consistent with what Melville does in his other works. To emphasize the meaning of *Bartleby* as Melville's personal careerist pathos ignores much of the rest of the story. It also tells us very little about the man Melville, the role of middling successful writers, the postal service, or any reasonably related topical matter. Indeed, as a document in self-pity the story tells us so little, and in such an irrelevant way, that it could well be dismissed by all but pedantic specialists in Melville. Since many good readers find the experience of the novella a moving one—I would argue that *Bartleby*, for reasons already suggested, is Melville's best work of fiction— we should not reduce it to an awkward footnote in a superficial case history of literary marketing. Biographical allegorizing, especially within a reductive psychological and social ideology, treats art as conspiratorial camouflage for self-pity and usually best fits bad writings by the most conventional people. Granted, biography done with social and psychological subtlety, and with a dramatic sense of eternal human predicaments, can be a fascinating and authentic art, but it will not serve as a complete substitute for other truths of the literary-philosophical mind, such as Melville's.

We should, then, acknowledge the story's own dialectic. While learned criticism may be indulged in wayward exposition and digressive little explorations, we need not follow it in playing

[16]Another quaint associational reading treats the substance of the story as the metaphor of "dead letters." Peter E. Fuchow, "Bartleby; Man and Metaphor," *Studies in Short Fiction*, V (Summer 1968), pp. 342-348.

[17]Merlin Bowen reasonably summarizes Bartleby's, and Melville's, attitude as resulting "from long contemplation of a pointless existence in a meaningless universe." *The Long Encounter* (Chicago, 1960), p. 133.

with little "keys" made out of source materials or stock mythologies or biographical clichés. We better serve the literature by asking significance than source. *Bartleby is*, and to understand the value of the perverse clerk must lead us through Melville's dialectic to the existential perversities in our culture.

3. *Again, the Good American*

Bartleby only contains one reasonably full character, the unnamed narrating attorney. Not only does all the story come from him but the emphasis upon his consciousness and self-argument means that he, not Bartleby, provides the problem of the story as well as its form.[18] The mysterious Bartleby, and the other materials such as the two minor scriveners, mostly provide occasions for the narrator's responses. We see what he sees but also what he fails to see, which comes out in Melville's emphasis upon the peculiar limitations of the narrating attorney in explaining and justifying himself. This self-rationalizing shows a pattern similar to what we found in *Benito Cereno* and *Billy Budd*. Bartleby does the refusing, the nay-saying, and not much more; the attorney does the explaining for both of them. Bartleby, I suggest, provides the specter of rebellious and irrational will whose very existence the narrating attorney denies. That there could be such a possibility as Bartleby, a forlorn refusal to abide by his version of sentimental reasonableness and pragmatic adjustment and repressive prudence, perplexes and haunts him. He feels compelled to explain away that perverse individual will and pessimistic sadness of his accusingly silent clerk.[19] That inability of the truth to speak—also represented by

[18]I grant that such terms as "form" and "structure" are dubious, usually meaning just mechanical pattern. For example, they are used in that way by Marvin Felheim, "Meaning and Structure in 'Bartleby'," *College English*, XXIII (February 1962), p. 365 ff.

[19]To Melville's silent figures such as Bartleby we might apply Ishmael's comment: "Seldom have I known any profound being that had anything to say to this world, unless forced to stammer out something by way of getting a living." *Moby Dick*, ed. Harrison Hayford and Herschel Parker (New York, 1967), p. 312.

Billy Budd's ignorance and stutter, by Benito Cereno's despairing quietness, by Babo's bitter silence, and by other silences in Melville's stories—points to the author's odd strategy. He aims at the devastatingly quiet truth by showing us the loquacious substitute for the truth.[20]

We thus find a systematically ironic analysis of the blandly benevolent rationalist. With *Bartleby's* attorney, as with *Benito Cereno's* Captain Delano, we see the practical optimist as representative liberal American. The Wall Street attorney, like the captains in Melville's other fictions, provides an image of a decent, well-meaning, rationalizing enforcer of established values.[21] Such figures miserably fail in a deeper and darker awareness of humanity, and in breaking out of the paradigmatic authority and order in which they comfortably reside. Melville thus indicts a major tradition of moral reasonableness in our time as well as in his time.

Before looking at the narrating attorney's self-arguments, we might briefly consider the scene of the story. "Wall Street" provides a metaphysical pun rather than an economic trope. Walls, dead walls of restriction and incomprehension, block everything. One side of the lawyer's chambers faces a white wall, the other side a black wall. But, in contrast to the whiteness in *Moby Dick* and the blackness in *Benito Cereno,* we have no moral black-white conflict, straight or inverted. We must understand imagery as it functions in the specific work before looking beyond to its larger significance. Here the white wall forms a stagnant "cistern" as entrapping as the black wall. Bartleby, who spends much of his time in "dead-wall reveries," and who is further walled into the attorney's private chamber and consciousness by a screen placed around him, represents a beyond black and white, good

---

[20]Even critics taking a narrow view of Melville's fictions note some similarities. See James E. Miller, Jr., for a comment on the relation of Benito Cereno and Bartleby. *A Reader's Guide to Herman Melville* (New York, 1962), p. 160.

[21]H. Bruce Franklin lists half a dozen similarities between Bartleby and Billy Budd, pp. 189-190, which suggests the other side of the parallel.

and evil, issue—a fundamental restriction of consciousness and relationship, the human walled-in-ness which transcends the usual moral terms.

The walls of the metaphoric abstract scene find other poetic extensions. Melville plays upon a series of analogies and allusions to other walls. Several refer to classic ruins—the futile dead walls that failed to keep civilization alive and human. The capping metaphor of walls of death comes from the exceptionally heavy and grim ones of the "Halls of Justice" which provide the final extension of the legal office of the main action. This, the New York "Tombs" prison, combines the facade of ancient civilization with modern law, restriction and punishment. Here Bartleby willfully dies. The tomb of Justice is compared, in monumental futility, to the Egyptian pyramids. Notes the narrator of the place, the "Egyptian character of that masonry weighed upon me with its gloom." The unusual order of the comparison, with the exotic aspect rather than the jailing aspect providing the cause of the gloom, suggests, as do other comparisons, that the ancient sense of order is the burden. The walled-in Wall Street lawyer, of course, fails to recognize himself as part of the walls of gloom and the mortuary process of deadening civilization.

As several commentators on *Bartleby* point out, the struggle against walls appears elsewhere in Melville. Ahab summarizes the most noted in *Moby Dick* in the remark that the "dead blind wall butts all inquiring heads at last."[22] This metaphysical malaise finds social ramifications in what Melville does emphasize about Wall Street—its restrictive multiplication of walled-in law offices and unresponsive lawyers. Not only dead laws about the dead, such as those of chancery by which the narrator makes much of his living, but the deadly legal logic, also practiced by the narrator, confines any fuller understanding of the forlorn

[22]*Moby Dick*, p. 427. The reference below to the mockery of law is, of course, to chapters 89 and 90 on antique whale laws.

human condition. Bartleby, a small wan Ahab, defiantly butts all such blind walls.

In most of his works, Melville mocks the legalistic mind, as in those humorous passages in *Moby Dick* on antique whale laws, in those harsh passages in *Billy Budd* on mutiny law, and in those dry passages in *Benito Cereno* on the laws punishing the rebellious slaves. Dead walls, dead laws, and "Dead Letters" merge into the mortuary monuments of imprisoning dead civilization in an incomprehensible world. The law, in its several senses, becomes a dead letter, deathly to human truth.[23]

Though lower-keyed in *Bartleby* than in *Moby Dick*, this play with the ramifying philosophical analogy characterizes Melville's mind. Such abstraction also applies to the characters. Bartleby is hardly "seen" except as a metaphysical problem and an "incurably forlorn" presence. The author even plays upon the abstractness of the scrivener; says the attorney, "had there been anything ordinarily human about him, doubtless I should have violently dismissed him from the premises." The point also makes ironic comment on the narrator if we see Bartleby as abstract personification of the attorney's own humanity.

This narrator paradoxically characterizes himself at the start as a reflective man and "an eminently *safe* man." His two "grand" qualities, he tells us, are "prudence" and "method." A commercial attorney, specializing in probate and rich men's bonds, he smugly associates himself with American greed and with the high opinion of John Jacob Astor. Protected by the prudential barriers of social and economic legalism, his office is less Bartleby's heritage than the attorney's own "retreat" from common humanity. For him, as for Captain Vere, law does not relate to morality; he lacks all passion for justice, without which law is mere formalism, and he does not, he tells us, "indulge in danger-

---

[23]My former colleague Charles Mitchell has extended some of my points on Melville's mocking "use of legal forms for the protection of evil." See "Melville and the Spurious Truth of Legalism," *Centennial Review*, XII (Winter 1968), pp. 110 ff.

ous indignation at wrongs and outrages." The attorney admits that he only came close to such feeling when they abolished his sinecure of Master in Chancery. Probate, traditionally and still one of the more lucrative of common legal exploitations, was also harshly satirized by other writers in Melville's time, such as Charles Dickens in *Bleak House,* which may well be a source for *Bartleby.*[24]

Not incidentally, the narrator as representative figure of a world of prudent privilege is also another of Melville's bachelors. He displays the genial rationality of bachelor Captain Delano and the ideology of tradition of bachelor Captain Vere. Only in *Bartleby* we find far more comedy, with the attorney self-indulgently admitting his "profound conviction that the easiest way of life is the best." Melville presents some of the consequent absurdities in the description of the grotesque office and staff. The attorney has long employed a pair of markedly irrational scriveners, Turkey and Nippers. Presented as Dickensian humor-caricatures, they provide comic foreshadowing of the lawyer's attempt to comfortably rationalize the irrational with Bartleby. One, a confirmed drunkard, works as a good copyist in the mornings but is of little use after his liquid lunch. The other, dyspeptic and ambitiously irritable in the mornings, resigns himself to productive tedium in the afternoons. Comfortably aware of their erratic behavior, the attorney turns it to his profitable ideology; since their "fits relieved each other" it provided "a good natural arrangement" for getting a day's work done. Thus conflicting individual motives manage to produce a parody of Adam Smith's general harmony and welfare. The attorney claims to have rationalized individual selfishness and madness into a utilitarian good—his.

[24]According to the note in the New Oxford Edition, *Bleak House* "was first published in monthly parts from March 1852 to September 1853. . . ." This well fits the probable time in which Melville was writing his story. Both the Chancery motif and the development of the scriveners suggest strong influence. While sources are rarely important, I suppose this one has been ignored for lesser sources because of the parochialism of American literary scholarship.

Turkey and Nippers reveal a startling, and often violently arrogant, self-regard in petty matters quite at odds with their menial roles—a comic expression of their dehumanization. But even this their absurdly methodological master rationalizes into advantage. When the new scrivener, Bartleby, joins them, he appears in his cadaverous withdrawal more sane than the office norm, until he appropriately refuses to allow himself to be completely absorbed into the madly rationalized self-interest of the master. Then the main problem for the narrator becomes how to deal with someone who cannot be manipulated by the selfish nexus. Here we see the deepest falsity of the self-interest rationalization, which goes beyond exploitation and mad accommodation to the falsification of human reality. Consequently, Bartleby's refusals drive the attorney to a threatening new awareness: for "the first time in my life . . . overpowering melancholy seized upon me. The bond of a common humanity now drew me irresistably to gloom." Bartleby's contrariety forces the attorney to recognize a whole side of life excluded by his optimistic self-interest. This genially selfish man with his comically smug certitudes "begins to stagger in his own plainest faith." Self-interest rests not in rationality but in piety. He even comes to suspect that somehow his madly defiant scrivener is right, that "all the justice and reason is on the other side"—as of course it is. The main force of the story comes from the attorney's various stratagems to reestablish his rationalized selfishness and prudently optimistic faith.

Thinking of sad and solitary Bartleby, the attorney moves from pity to melancholy to fear to repulsion in the classic sentimentality-to-hostility responses to victims which most of us practice. Though the narrator soon works his way back into his usual "prudential feeling," he has been on the threshhold of the bitter knowledge that human suffering is less to be understood in terms of "inherent selfishness" than as a more fundamental "hopelessness." Such awareness, in Melville's usual anti-Christian irony, "disqualified" the attorney, for that Sunday at least, "from churchgoing."

The attorney's rationality repeatedly comes up against something deeper, "some paramount consideration" in his scrivener's behavior that makes his denials "irreversible." That paramount force must be defined as individual *will*. We see its logic in odd ways. In his fantastic rationality, the attorney debates with himself as to why Bartleby apparently subsists only on the little cakes called "ginger nuts." They are hot and spicy and Bartleby is anything but. Therefore, only some strange preference can explain his living on them. And that explains nothing except the primacy of preference itself. So, too, with Bartleby's "I prefer not to."

To rid himself of the irrationality of preference, of human will, the narrator persuasively tells his defiant copyist to leave, and generously appeals to his selfishness by offering a present of money (later he admits to himself that it was a "bribe"). Then he congratulates himself on his "masterly management" in getting rid of the "incubus" that defied his decency and reasons: "I assumed the ground that depart he must. . . ." But his little demon operates on preferences, not assumptions, and will not leave. Desperate, the rationalist then carries his calculated decency contrary to the fact; he will force Bartleby to leave by assuming, in front of him, that he has already left. To the unintentionally humorous narrator, "It was hardly possible that Bartleby could withstand such an application of the doctrine of assumptions." But the perverse little devil replies, for the seventeenth time, "I would prefer *not* to."

Bartleby chooses the right tactic to confront the attorney who can never quite act with brutal directness against the disarming "wonderful mildness" of his scrivener. As now generally recognized in American protest movements, such highly civil disobedience provides an effective strategy of moral resistance to the would-be decent and rational "liberal." (Its ineffectiveness against the violent or otherwise illiberal necessarily raises not only other questions but harsher responses.) As the attorney says, "Nothing so aggravates an earnest person as passive resistance." Such focused aggravation provides the therapy of civil disobedience rather more successfully than the morality and love propounded by the usual Ghandian ideologies. The attorney cannot directly call the police since to maintain himself he must claim to act within the limits of the decent and rational mind—that is his faith—but he can move away and later let somebody else call the police to haul Bartleby away. Contemporary parallels should be evident.

When his doctrine of assumptions does not rid him of his demon of a scrivener, the narrator falls into despair. So he looks into "Edwards on the Will" and "Priestley on Necessity." Bartleby, we see, serves as *the* intellectual issue for the civilized attorney, the root perplexity of the benevolent rationalist who wishes not to meet rebellious irrationality by personal decision but by bookish moral logic. Learned arguments, however, will not answer the problem since the narrator concludes from his theological and scientific sources (both necessitarian, though the first dour and the latter benign) that his scrivener troubles "had been predestined from eternity." He then decides, with a religious smugness like the good Protestant Captain Delano, that the deity will take care of all for his clerk has been "billeted upon [him] for some mysterious purpose of all wise Providence." But as usual, Protestant determinism and morality seem especially vulnerable to social pressure—the deity is so far away—and the narrator uses the disapproval of his neighboring lawyers as justification for escaping Bartleby and metaphysical necessity by moving to another office. Not only does he hope to leave behind "such perverseness—such unreasonableness," which has become a comic contagion in his office with everyone suddenly expressing preferences, he also flees a larger awareness: "Presentiments of strange discoveries hovered around me." Providence and prudence combine, finally, to justify limiting human awareness and response. Concludes the attorney, "My conscience justified me."

Bartleby, forcibly removed by the police from the attorney's former premises, is charged with vagrancy. In more of his comical reasoning, the attorney grants that Bartleby really suffers from being insufficiently vagrant. His own vagrant thoughts show a preoccupation with Bartleby, as if the scrivener were still a secret part of himself. Some critics therefore describe the tale as a study in "schizophrenia."[25] Perhaps more important here than that rather uncertain clinical category would be the related literary motif of the "double." Melville often uses such a pattern of matched-and-split characters: Vere-Budd, Ahab-Ishmael, Cereno-Babo, as well as the companion pairs in his adventure stories.[26] But in *Bartleby* the psychological splitting or doubling of character to dramatize an essentially internal conflict is heightened almost to the degree that we find in the classic instances of Dostoyevsky's *The Double* and Conrad's *The Secret Sharer*. In Melville's story the combination of the pragmatically moral attorney and the mutedly demonic scrivener dramatizes the ideological conflict appropriate to the decent American, the conforming but conscience stricken attorney. Bartleby's small perverse will takes precisely the modest and even decorous tone appropriate to the prudently rationalized goodness of the representative Wall Street lawyer. The scrivener provides the human

[25]The story has been described as a study in "schizophrenia" by two of the better biographical critics: Newton Arvin, *Herman Melville* (New York, 1950), p. 244, and Richard Chase, *Herman Melville* (New York, 1949), p. 143. Mordecai Marcus, "Melville's Bartleby as a Psychological Double," *College English*, XXIII (February 1962), pp. 365-368, gives one version of the "double" theme but collapses it into a socio-economic emphasis on "Wall Street." For a discussion of the "double" as an ironist's technique for playing the demonic against common morality, see Kingsley Widmer, "Conrad's Pyrrhic *Victory*," *Twentieth Century Literature*, V (Summer 1959).

[26]Richard Abcarian, following the often suggestive Richard Chase, rightly notes parallels between Bartleby and his attorney. "The World of Love and the Spheres of Fright: Melville's 'Bartleby'," *Studies in Short Fiction*, I (Spring 1964), pp. 207-215.

completion, the rage to the restraint, the covert rebellion to the conviction that "the easiest way of life is the best," the assertion of human preference against depersonalized assumptions, and the melancholy pessimism to balance the bland optimism.

Such doubling provides a grotesque version of the great Faust theme in which the duality of consciousness requires the spirit of negation. The image of the ever-resistant clerk completes the human depth of the ever-adapting attorney.[27] For we must repeatedly recognize that the attorney literally demands the confrontation with Bartleby. Though on the surface horrified by the clerk's defiance, he suddenly acknowledges: "I burned to be rebelled against again." The demon of denial is essential to human existence.

The attorney thus becomes the victim of his victim, reversing roles to read his own copy, slinking away from his own door for fear of meeting his defiant scrivener, even threatened in his own deepest faith. Yet he cannot stop himself from trying to fit Bartleby into his narrowly calculated and walled-in world. At one point the attorney convinces himself that Bartleby must be "demented"; as if to confirm this judgment, the scrivener quits the last copying which provided, until then, some rationale for keeping the otherwise insubordinate clerk. Of Bartleby's new refusal, the attorney righteously demands "And what is the reason?" Bartleby coolly replies, "Do you not see the reason for yourself?" None is self-evident but, with comic alacrity, the attorney "instantly" comes up with a reason to justify the fantastic behavior he just previously denounced as demented. He decides to assume that Bartleby has "temporarily impaired his vision" by his copy work. (Melville, the biographers tell us, had trouble with his own eyesight—apparently psychosomatic—during his writing and proofreading, but to turn from the character to the author here would again be to confuse the meaning of a

[27]Chase shrewdly suggests that both Bartleby and the attorney must be understood as parts of Melville and of the obsessional father-son pattern evident in so many of his works. *Herman Melville,* pp. 143-149.

motif with its possible source.[28]) The attorney's bad-eyesight rationalization for Bartleby's refusal seems kindly and useful; it also totally lacks support in any fact or assertion and appears especially gratuitous at that moment. The decent rationalist will produce an assumption, even one contrary to reason and evidence, to explain away rebellious behavior, no matter what.

Shortly later the attorney asks Bartleby to do something not at all dependent on his eyes. The scrivener again refuses. Then the attorney hopefully suggests to Bartleby the possibility of his doing copying sometime in the future when his eyes should be normal. The scrivener, totally ignoring the narrator's proffered rationalization for his refusal, simply refuses for all time to copy. (Obviously, here Bartleby cannot, contrary to fashionable criticism, be equated directly with Melville-as-writer who was just embarking on a long series of stories at the time of writing *Bartleby*.) Another reason up, another reason down; the perverse negation remains, and so does the gulf between the narrator's utilitarian reasoning and Bartleby's defiant choosing.

Melville, as I suggested at the start of this discussion, parallels Dostoyevsky in mocking the doctrine that men find their truest motivation in enlightened self-interest. That emphasis appears quite clearly in the story. Absolutist Bartleby, who asserts the freedom of the will but declines to gives it any specific reasons or moral values, lacks any recognizable selfishness. Repeatedly through the story, the attorney triumphantly resorts to offers of money, better employment, letters of recommendation, travel, a home, friendship—any selfish desire with which the enlightened human being might be manipulated—but Bartleby remains unamenable to the calculus of all such selfishness. With Bartleby, unlike the other scriveners in his office, the attorney cannot

---

[28]Richard Fogle notes the confusion in critics taking the "eyesight" metaphor as autobiography, among other reasonable objections to such allegorizing, in *Melville's Shorter Tales* (Norman, Okla., 1960), pp. 14-27. Like the attorney, however, Fogle at one point makes Bartleby the "victim of his environment" and at another insists on "predestination."

create a utilitarian pattern by mixing advantage with weakness. Therefore he prudently attempts to incorporate the perverse negations of his clerk within his accommodating philosophy by raising the issue to a moral level. As long as Bartleby, however insubordinate, will copy, the attorney will bear with him so as to demonstrate his liberal tolerance of the unfortunate and thus "cheaply produce a delicious self-approval" of "conscience." What a devastating admission! Those things beyond one's control can still be turned to profit by patronizingly adapting them for moral self-aggrandizement.

When Bartleby refuses to copy any more, the attorney attempts the balm of a higher morality, again to his own advantage. He stays his rage against Bartleby by recalling a parabolic situation. "I remember the tragedy of the unfortunate Adams and the still more unfortunate Colt . . . and how poor Colt, being dreadfully incensed by Adams, and imprudently permitting himself to get wildly excited, was at unawares hurried into his fatal act." Here Melville apparently adapts a murder of his time to comically expose his rationalizing attorney. Notice, for example, how the character reads murderous rage as mere imprudence. This man has lost all sense of the passions of life.

The attorney adds a theological moral to the fable by remembering "the divine injunction: 'A new commandment give I unto you, that ye love one another'." Here the Gospel drama of love to overcome sin ("this old Adam of resentment" in Melville's curious reduction) comes out as clever Wall Street caution.

Yes, this it was that saved me. Aside from higher considerations, charity often operates as a vastly wise and prudent principle—a great safeguard to its possessor. . . . No man, that ever I heard of, ever committed a diabolical murder for sweet charity's sake. Mere self-interest, then, if no better motive can be enlisted, should, especially with high-tempered men, prompt all beings to charity and philanthropy. At any rate, upon the occasion in question, I strove to draw my exasperated feelings towards the scrivener by benevolently construing his conduct. Poor fellow, poor fellow! thought I, he don't mean anything; and besides, he has seen hard times, and ought to be indulged.

This passage provides a good example of Melville's concern and craft: the revealing "prudent" again, the moralistic self-congratulation, the pompousness of "benevolently construing," the patronizing assumption of environmental causes ("hard times"), the contemptuous use of pity to dismiss ("poor fellow . . . he don't mean anything"), and the whole argument for making love and forgiveness into a sort of cheap insurance policy. Goodness as "mere self-interest" reveals the obtuseness of such rationality and the brutality of such decency.

It might be countered in defense of enlightened self-interest that we do see the attorney as proof of the applicability of the doctrine, on its selfish side anyway. Certainly we should appreciate the irony of the selfish attorney defending the high morality of self-interest. This shows a common ploy of those arguing for such views of human motivation; they assure us they have examined their own hearts and found selfishness there, so why don't you admit yours? But that falsifies the point. The rebuttal, not directly made in the story, must be that self-interest serves to excuse and obscure other things to be found in the heart.

Part of what the attorney is covering up is his common humanity with Bartleby. As usual, Melville not only displays some subtlety but gives us an ambiguous reversal in the story. The attorney, in spite of his smug utilitarianism, has become deeply involved with his perverse scrivener: "strange to say—I tore myself away from him whom I had so longed to be rid of." And though he has gotten away from his demon, by his rationalizations in pseudo-morality and moving his office, he persists, in a mixture of obscurely kindly and guilty concern, in visiting Bartleby in prison and dispensing prudent charity. We need not rehearse here all his stratagems of moral bribes and appeals to further self-interest to also realize that in their very comic excess something else appears. For a subterranean feeling develops in the narrator, ranging from his earlier responses to Bartleby as the most "forlorn of humanity" through his fears of larger presentiments to an intermittent recognition of a "common" condition with the scrivener to a final sense of heroic suffering.

In his visits to Bartleby in prison, the attorney finds him both more adamant and more accusing than ever. The ex-scrivener refuses to eat, to change, to ameliorate his forlornness—refuses not to prefer not to. Staring at yet more walls, Bartleby says to the good citizen who comfortably accepts the walled-in life: "I know you . . . and I want nothing to say to you." Moved by such solitary resistance, the attorney feels Bartleby to be some sacrificial figure amidst the thieves and murders. After Bartleby's final denial, he is found fetally lying dead in the Egyptian courtyard of the jail. The narrator then pronounces the epitaph: Bartleby sleeps, he says, "With kings and counsellors." The phrase probably comes from Job's rebellious curses against an unjust and inexplicable cosmos.[29] Bartleby properly belongs, then, as a hero of such a suffering and defiant world view. And with such heightening, the majesty of negation and the wisdom of defeat should be unmistakeable to the narrator and to the reader.[30]

But only temporarily for the narrator. We must consider again his final fervent paragraph about Bartleby having once worked in the Dead Letter Office. However interpreted, some astute

[29]3:14 (KJV). A number of critics, following the suggestion in my earlier essay on Bartleby, now cite Job as the probable source of the attorney's statement. We might further see the attorney as a sort of comic Job in a Godless universe.

[30]Norman Springer draws heavily upon my earlier study of the story but objects, mistakenly, that I hold the narrator to be redeemed. "Bartleby and the Terror of Limitation," PMLA, LXXX (September 1965), p. 410 (note). Some of Springer's remarks on the attorney's character are apt but he wrongly assumes that the narrator's self-interest and charity are in conflict and postulates a Christian moral which is contradictory to the story, antithetical to Melville, and quite misses the nihilistic logic.

readers find this conclusion to be badly anticlimactic.[31] Certainly such an ending once again explains away Bartleby as the victim of "hard times" and pity-engendering circumstances, and so leaves him charitably patronized in memory. And the final eulogistic line, universalizing the moral of forlornness, suggests thick Victorianism: "Ah, Bartleby! Ah, Humanity!" (A famous contemporary American novelist once told me he was writing a similar sort of novella but had avoided Melville's "mistake" of forgetting his ironic tone and making a sentimental generality.[32]) Surely some preparation for this concluding line appears in the narrator's increasingly impassioned view of Bartleby, in spite of his comfortably selfish ideology. The humanistic beatification of Bartleby, forlorn saint of defiance in the American walled world of legalism and commerce and utilitarian morality, does not violate our cumulative sense of his significance. And "humanity" in that last line must be allowed a similar resonance to what Melville, a believer in the profundity of defeat rather than the American dream of success, wrote in another story: "Humanity, thou strong thing, I worship thee, not in the laureled victor, but in this vanquished one."[33] This is not only tragic principle but, considering most of what success in America amounts to, the minimum moral response to our realities.

We must also remember that the final sentiments come not directly from the author but from his mockingly treated attorney-narrator. To his walled-in awareness, Bartleby and humanity remain inexplicable, unacceptable. Though he half-consciously detects some awesome and awful significance in his demon of a scrivener, he still remains the benevolent rationalist and arch-representative of American optimistic and prudent self-interest.

[31]The failure of the ending is cogently pointed out by Charles G. Hoffmann, "The Shorter Fictions of Herman Melville," *South Atlantic Quarterly*, LII (July 1953), p. 420.

[32]The novelist was Saul Bellow, in his less conservative days. He was apparently speaking of *Seize the Day*.

[33]"Norfolk Isle and the Chola Widow," *Complete Stories*, p. 94.

The attorney's final statement, therefore, must be read with some irony; it marks his moralizing and rationalizing failure to understand Bartleby; he makes a last sentimental gesture when confronted with overwhelming resistance to his faith.

Are we to take the narrator's preceding remarks about Bartleby as Dead Letter clerk as sentimentality or irony? The attorney gives a maudlin hypothetical picture of Bartleby as Dead Letter clerk: "from out the folded paper the pale clerk takes a ring—the finger it was meant for, perhaps, moulders in the grave." He thus attempts to explain Bartleby as a victim of unfortunate circumstances and depressing knowledge. This continues the incomprehension of the attorney earlier in the story and his dubious tactics for salving his conscience. The indulgence in mawkish speculations buries any deeper insight and response. The Dead Letter anecdotes more explain away than respond to Bartleby's defiance of the narrator's self-interest ideology and dead-wall way of life.

The ending of Bartleby can be read as sentimental, though it then becomes a failure in the story—a collapse into maudlin style and irrelevant epilogue. Ironically, however, the ending would continue the themes of the novella and its mockery of bland consciousness. Perhaps we should allow for some of both. Melville, self-made and self-doubting critic of our benevolent rationalism and faith in comfortable and optimistic manipulation, may both perceive ambiguities here and falter in them. The ending could be seen as sentimentally bad in style and still serve the story as final ironic comment. However, we should not reduce this to authorial pathos. The writer who demonically recreated the big white God as a whale did not make the absurdly sainted Bartleby just as an image of self-bathos, though a bit may insinuate itself. Far more importantly than private statement, *Bartleby* reveals the confession of a decent, prudent, rational "liberal" who finds in his chambers of consciousness the incomprehensible, perverse, irrational demon of denial, and of his own denied humanity. The attorney must be viewed partly as a sympathetically treated figure (again, like Captain Delano in *Benito Cereno*). He does his best and attempts to exorcise that rebellious and infuriating image with conventional assumptions, authority, utility, legalism, religious orthodoxy, prudent charity, flight, and, at the end, sentimental reverence. The enigma remains, and the accusation, not least because the narrator never adequately confronts the meaning of Bartleby and his refusals, never changes his view and way of life.[34]

The modest demon of defiant and pessimistic will, he who endlessly "prefers not to" do and accept what we pretend to be the normative, legal and walled, conditions effectively questions our civilized order. But it is the narrator, that good American, not Bartleby, that enigmatic wisdom, who ends as the pathetically grotesque figure with all his rationalized self-interest and prudentially twisted virtue. The attempt to wryly force benevolent American rationalism to an awareness of our forlorn and walled-in humanity provides the larger purpose of the tale.[35]

4. *The Perverse Artist*

In mocking the rationality and morality of enlightened self-interest, Melville, with his usual involution, presents the fable from the benevolent rationalist's point of view. A more rebellious author probably would have presented the story and argument from Bartleby's point of view. The attorney's sentimental and prudent sensibility certainly mutes some of the extremity. Still, Bartleby, like the similar figures in *Benito Cereno* and *Billy Budd*, willfully goes to his death. This assertion of the will by the destruction of the will seems, above all, to characterize

[34]My negative interpretation of the attorney contrasts with those who take the ending as a change in character in which his "exposure" to Bartleby "eventually leads to his salvation." John Bernstein, *Pacifism and Rebellion in the Writings of Herman Melville* (The Hague, Netherlands, 1964), p. 171.

[35]In one of the more confused comments on the story, the "dead letters" are equated with Melville's novels and the story is said to be about "the mystery of life." R. W. B. Lewis, *Trials of the Word* (New Haven, Conn., 1965), p. 42.

those views usually called nihilistic. We must recall, of course, Bartleby's function as the attorney's double and demon: the benevolent rationalist, and his restricted view of life, calls forth the nihilism.

In *Notes from the Underground,* Dostoyevsky presents issues similar to those of Melville's *Bartleby* but from the defiant clerk's point of view. For Dostoyevsky, the "reader" (the "gentlemen" often directly addressed in the monologue) provides the benevolent rationalist, the equivalent responses to those of Melville's attorney. To center, as Dostoyevsky does, on the consciousness of the perverse clerk makes more emphatic the destructive and "sick" qualities—the spitefulness, the exacerbated self-consciousness, the masochistic desire for suffering. The sick despair and self-torturings involved in Melville's more indirect and abstract story remain less identifiable and obtrusive. Where Dostoyevsky becomes frenzied about the negations, Melville stays within wry pathos. Artistically, we might hold that Melville was the more successful. *Bartleby* remains a tale, rather than falling over into philosophical monologue and illustrative melodrama. Yet the reader of the interpretations of both novellas, and of the history of criticism around them, will also be aware of a reversing irony. Dostoyevsky's *Notes from the Underground* is far more often recognized for something like what it says than is Melville's *Bartleby*.[36] Another encouragement to nihilism: even in literature, disproportion, destructiveness, extremity seem necessary to effectively make a point.

Something more should be noted about this extremity in relation to the arguments against self-interest. Obviously, to make plausible extreme behavior itself provides part of the argument. However, it can be, and often is, said of Dostoyevsky's man-from-underground that his arguments against "advantage" seem disingenuous justifications of his pathology. That clerk

---

[36]For example, portentous and vague analogies with later existentialist writers provide the only interpretation in Maurice Friedman, *Problematic Rebel* (New York, 1963), pp. 77-98.

takes a certain selfish advantage from his self-exacerbation (he thus shapes an otherwise empty life), in his frenzied justifications (he can't help himself and so makes a philosophy of his sickness), or at least in sheer style (his inverted romanticism gives him an anti-style as substitute for a lifestyle). In Melville's story, the clerk is so artfully abstracted, and we so focus on the limitations of the narrator, that no pathology or advantage of Bartleby can become the issue. Yet because of this Melville's critics, rather more than Dostoyevsky's, tend to obscure the argument by talking about the allegory of the artist and other parochial irrelevancies. Which author, then, best succeeds with his demonish little clerk taking liberal-rationalist sensibility down the dark path?

I suspect that liberal-rationalism generally responds to behavior and views not readily identifiable as "self-interested" as if they were darkly nihilistic. Thus Dostoyevsky's underground clerk, even Melville's Bartleby, appears either nihilistically mad or practicing a perverse selfishness. That last won't do. To be pertinent, "self-interest" must be a relatively limited and unperverse choice. To say that everything a man does or doesn't do—from suicide to the very arguing against self-interest—can be seen as a variant of rational selfishness must obliterate a genuine issue. True, Dostoyevsky, in the passage quoted earlier, speaks of defiant and capricious freedom as the "one most advantageous advantage." But that is a witty paradox, a twist of the argument against itself. True, Bartleby allows his attorney to propose self-interested reasons for the scrivener's refusals—"Do you not see the reason for yourself?"—but they in no way apply to his refusals, nor change them. Neither resisting clerk can be adequately explained by any of the usual rationalized advantages.

As a social morality and political assumption the self-interest doctrine requires that the rationalized selfishness be readily recognizable and repeatable. For me to justify my calculated selfishness as reasonable and good means that you, and most others, must be able to do the same. Like a scientific verification (to which it may have some historical affinity), the self-interest must be generally available and repeatable. All clerks and attorneys, or businessmen and proletarians, or whatever, should be able to find and act upon the common selfishness or advantage. Like the traditional idealist notion of The Good, of which enlightened self-interest is a perverse twisting, one need only rightly see his selfish interest in order to beneficently choose it.

The perverse clerks of Dostoyevsky and Melville hardly allow any such normative possibilities. But they do raise grave doubts that men would choose their own advantage. Not only are most men really unable to calculate their own selfishness, they do not desire it. Even if they could and did, we are left with the perplexity as to how a generally acknowledged evil, selfishness, becomes a higher social good, rational self-interest. That certainly provides a weird chapter in the history of Western moral intelligence. The classical economic motivation of private pursuit of wealth producing public beneficence, a view which Dostoyevsky and Melville seem to clearly mock, appears mad in its emphasis upon competition rather than cooperation producing social harmony. No better, of course, is the argument that violent class interest, such as the advantage of proletarians (which must be calculated for them by turncoat bourgeois intellectuals), will produce an unselfish social change and result in a classless good society. The revolutionary inversion of a dubious dogma may not come out any better than the original selfishness, though one can sympathize with the desires to have things the other way around for awhile. Neither profit-competition nor social-class warfare seem persuasive when we examine, as do Dostoyevsky and Melville, the basic logic of self-interest. It then becomes hard to escape the conclusion that ancient moralists had the better arguments in their denunciations of selfishness. That appears to be what Dostoyevsky returns to. Melville seems to suggest something even more devastating: enlightened self-interest depends on a providential order—a secular masquerade of authoritarian magic, even in Marx—and that won't do once one recognizes, in proper dead-wall reveries, that this is a "meaningless" universe.

Most thoughtful people, I suppose, now recognize the drastic inadequacies of the grosser forms of the appeal to self-interest. A decent market-place certainly does not result from the primary quest for profits. Balancing interests—the "pluralist" model of democracy—hardly produces a community any more than the dominance of some groups' interests over all others. Pursuing the American "national interest" hardly suggests a freer world or a better America. Revolutionary changes for the better hardly seem likely from the resentful violence of class interests. Though official, popular, and lethal, these derivations from the self-interest view hardly get at the heart of it. What Dostoyevsky and Melville suggest is an even larger question: By what selfishness would a man choose to live?[37]

The answer must be "none." No plausible calculus of self-interest answers such crucial questions, no rationalized advantage justifies life. Can anyone really think that authentic existence, or a good society, or a desirable lifestyle could be based in anything reasonably explicable as self-interest? The "gentlemen" Dostoyevsky's man-from-underground addresses, Bartleby's attorney, and the audiences both authors direct their ironies at, seemed to have thought so. And is not the contemporary, enlightened reader still one of them? The thrust of the dramatic arguments seems aimed at what we would call a "liberal" reader, a benevolent rationalist of self-interest ideology.

[37]Of my earlier essay, Professor Mario L. D'Avanzo writes that he accepts the "perceptive interpretation of the narrator as a benevolent rationalist. However, his focus on Bartleby himself is inadequate, for the scrivener stands for more than perversity and perverse negation; there is method and logic to his apparent madness. Mr. Widmer's commentary I find the best intratextual criticism of 'Bartleby' but . . . severely limited." "Melville's 'Bartleby' and Carlyle," Bartleby, ed. Vincent, p. 195 (note B). While I appreciate the compliments, and here try to further explain the significance of Bartleby, I do not understand why D'Avanzo pursues the counter-argument and has Melville, now following Carlyle, "dramatizing the heroism of the man of letters" (p. 138).

Bartleby and *Notes from the Underground* provide major documents of "modernism." The authors perform as peculiarly contentious, extreme, subversive versions of the "artist." No shamans or bards or reporters or mythmakers, these labyrinthine and tormented philosophers seem impelled to do dialectical battle with the dominant rational and moral consciousness. Certainly this results in a limited and peculiar artistry, a rational irrationalism and destructive creativity which ends in near pathological portrayals and guilty paradoxes and nihilistic conclusions. But the passion for negation includes a powerful moral, Bartleby's "I prefer not to." That ethic of resistance remains the imperative of all dissenting scriveners. We learn from Bartleby that when confronting a false consciousness and the walled-in life of our mass technological bureaucracies we must refuse to acquiesce, even if we have to "prefer not to be a little reasonable." To do that takes a nihilistic awareness—nothing less will do—and Bartleby is a saint of such continuing refusal.

CHAPTER FIVE

CONCLUSION:
BEYOND NIHILISM?

Melville's Ishmael dryly comments that there are times "when a man takes this whole universe for a vast practical joke."[1] Some such expression of nihilistic awareness seems essential to Melville. When not harshly destroying innocence with Billy Budd or renouncing the blackness of life with Benito Cereno or resisting unto nothingness with Bartleby, the universe can at times be coolly comic. It can also be utterly savage, as with Melville's *Confidence Man* where the earnest old man, and the reader, end "left in the dark" with a bad smell.[2] The joke without a joker takes form in the deceptively promising appearances, the tortured myths of the past, and the diabolical masquerades—three versions of the same falsity of meaning which Melville invariably undercuts. For Melville, as for many other inverted romantics of the past century, one plays, in imitation of the non-existent deity-joker, with meanings and reasonings and sanctities to find being in nothingness.

The evidence for Melville-as-nihilist, the only attitude that makes sense of much of his work, seems overwhelming, for those willing to apprehend it, and one cannot easily go beyond it. To call someone a nihilist, of course, often amounts to hurling an

[1] *Moby Dick*, ed. Harrison Hayford and Herschel Parker (New York, 1967), p. 195. There are many similar remarks in Melville.

[2] *The Confidence Man* (New York, 1964), p. 260. I originally planned to include a detailed discussion of this novel but that might constitute a gratuitous elaboration of Melville's nihilistic emphasis, even though the Timonism has the "positive" moral that we should not be taken in by the "con" games.

epithet or curse. But we can discuss very little with those who insist on equating nihilism with evil, not least because the nihilist is vehemently reacting against evil. For a little more than a century now, at least since Turgenev portrayed ardently negative Yevgeny Bazarov as a nihilist, the term has focused a major subject as well as attitude in our literature.[3] Certainly there were also nihilists who threw bombs, in idealistic though finally ineffective response to vicious autocracy.[4] (Whether that was consistent with nihilism, or whether they should have thrown more bombs, could be debated.) There were also less active nihilists, such as Nietzsche, whose violence was mostly literary. He attempted to philosophize, as he put it, with a hammer, partly because the accepted pieties in a world in which God was dead were so pernicious—"How much blood and horror lies behind all 'good things'!"[5] As I understand him, he saw several nihilisms. The overwhelming one was the character of Western civilization, and those ostensibly defending it, in its destruction of all values. The point is still appropriate—as, indeed, was the way of Nietzsche's and Melville's contemporary Rimbaud in announcing "The Age of Assassins!" For Nietzsche, the proper counterresponse was also nihilistic—the intellectual as gaily serious destroyer. So nihilism in the nineteenth century develops into a self-conscious role and style, becomes a culture.

Certainly nihilism became a major part of the literary-philosophical tradition usually called "modernism." Whether in

[3] I have not been able to find a use of "nihilism" in a modern sense prior to that in *Fathers and Sons* (1861) but there may well be some since the essential attitude is a "classic" response.

[4] There have been many discussions of the nihilist-terrorist political movement of Russian radical students, of which the most recent I have seen is the rather snide portrayal of Ronald Hingley, *Nihilists* (New York, 1969). Some of the perplexities, and resulting confusions, posed by such nihilistic movements for the liberal moralist are raised by Albert Camus, *The Rebel* (New York, 1956).

[5] *The Genealogy of Morals*, tr. Francis Golffing (New York, 1956), p. 194. I believe Joseph Heller has rightly, though antagonistically, perceived one main emphasis of such nihilists—the raising of an unending oppositional dialectic to an absolute—in *Dialectics and Nihilism* (Amherst, 1966).

manner the "ontological absurd" of the existentialists, or the emphatic "nonsense" of the Dadaists, or the many related ways of countering falsity and "meaninglessness" with moral negation and intellectual destructiveness, we can readily find the continuities of nihilism.[6] It was essential even to D. H. Lawrence, in some ways one of the most positive of twentieth century writer-prophets, to emphasize such a way down to wisdom: "once we are driven on to nihilism we may find a way through."[7] It was this same "modernist" tradition of sensibility which revived and gave new dimensions to Herman Melville and raised him to the status of the classic American author, with all the cultural piety and institutional mis-emphasis that go with it. There is a lovely nihilistic irony to all this.

Yet another irony might be found in the major current use of accusations of nihilism. They are vociferously applied to the young, and their mentors, cultivated in that "modernist" tradition and its nineteenth century forerunners. The century only carried us, and nihilism, in a circle, back to the ardently negative young rebels.[8] For any definition of nihilism perhaps we should not lose sight of that simply recurrent human reality—the vital desire to angrily negate things as they are.

The nihilistic cultural tradition certainly contains much more than that—after all, it is probably one of the basic life-attitudes—but it is difficult to more exactly define nihilism because hardly

[6]Some of the recent discussions of modernism, such as Renato Poggioli, *The Theory of the Avant-Garde* (Cambridge, Mass., 1969), suggest the broad generalization, though Camus and others have rightly carried it back much further in time.

[7]*Fantasia of the Unconscious* (London, 1933), p. 64. This attitude and its effects on literature are discussed at considerable length in Kingsley Widmer, *The Art of Perversity: D. H. Lawrence's Shorter Fictions* (Seattle, Washington, 1962). Lawrence, of course, was one of the first to insist on the destructiveness as well as genius of Melville in *Studies in Classic American Literature*.

[8]A representative example of the denunciations may be found in Lewis S. Feuer, *The Conflict of Generations* (New York, 1969). For a counter-polemic, see Kingsley Widmer, "Father and Son Destroyers," *The Nation*, 208 (May 5, 1969), 575-6, and, more broadly, "Why Dissent Turns Violent," *Nation*, 208 (April 7, 1969) and "Rebellion as Education," *Nation*, 208 (April 28, 1969).

anyone defends it as such. That puts the anti-nihilists in the rather awkward position of either attacking almost nothing and no one or putting down that which everyone agrees is bad, and therefore saying almost nothing. Such a sorry intellectual state might encourage one to charitably improve things a bit by saying a good word for nihilism. And considering most of the anti-nihilists—if, like them, we may be allowed *ad hominem* argument—there must be considerable to be said for the nihilists.

The most recent study at hand which tries to define nihilism starts out by positing it as that view in which "it makes no difference what we do" and to which "nothing is worth anything."[9] The obvious difficulty with this definition is that no one seems to hold such a view. It would be utterly foolish to do so since, by definition, it would not make any difference and would be worthless even if one held what one cannot hold. As usual, anti-nihilism so mis-states the issue as not to find a serious antagonist.

Several later definitions by the same philosopher seem more possible. There exists an ancient and serious tradition, he says, of nihilistic thought which holds in effect that a "rejuvenation of the human spirit is possible only through a complete destruction of the decadent present."[10] "Complete destruction," of course, mis-states the matter. As anyone who has attempted a little destroying knows, it is a rigorously discriminating process. With so much deserving to be destroyed, selection and action take an exceedingly incisive and limiting effort. More plausibly restated: "Nihilism is fundamentally an attempt to overcome or to repudiate the past on behalf of an unknown and unknowable but hoped-for future." Since nihilism is also part of the past, again we must qualify this to a very partial repudiation. But the definition does suggest that the nihilist attacks the past not for its pastness but for its utilization as justifying something which he finds dubious in the present. The nihilist, then, believes that

---

[9]Stanley Rosen, *Nihilism: A Philosophical Essay* (New Haven, 1969), p. xiii.
[10]Rosen, p. 105. The restatement quoted below is from p. 140.

if the historical-mythic sanction of, say, an institution—a concentration camp, a slave ship, an educational bureaucracy, a government—were broken the offending thing might be considerably changed. That seems eminently reasonable, though anti-nihilistic objections could be made that the rejection includes extreme consequences (as does the continued existence of the institution) or that for effectiveness some substitute instead of mere rejection should be offered. (The nihilist could easily counter that we reject a lie, a poison or a crime in its own right, and that positive amelioration often ends up reenforcing the bad rather than replacing it.) The rest of the definition oddly suggests that the future should be known or knowable, not just hoped-for. But that only reveals the arrogance of anti-nihilists, who demand of nihilists what they cannot reasonably furnish themselves.

But even granting such a definition, we have a problem putting together nihilism's mixture of negation and hopefulness. For is not nihilism based in despair? Our philosopher answers with some rather nihilistic paradoxes of his own: "The nihilist hopes for despair in order to be free for the possibility of hope"; and "The nihilist perseveres in the face of despair . . . because the worthlessness of all reasons is understood by him as freedom."[11] Thus we see that even to the anti-nihilist, nihilism depends on positive values such as freedom and hope, even amidst meaninglessness and despair. Nihilism, then, always contains self-transcendence and itself points beyond nihilism. Abstractly at least, our question (Beyond nihilism?) is answerable, and nihilism affirmable.

Haggling over definitions should not lead us to forget that any attitude plausibly described as nihilism must probably be

---

[11]Rosen, p. 142. See also the Christian polemic of Helmut Thielicke, *Nihilism* (New York, 1961), p. 28, which grants that modern nihilism is far different from hopelessness since it is driven by a "will to truth." Another philosopher, Hans Jonas, posits close connections between nihilism and the most extreme positive assertions of values such as gnosticism, *The Phenomenon of Life* (New York, 1966), pp. 231 ff.

recognized as extreme and quite possibly as destructive, but extreme attitudes may sometimes be not only appropriate but the only decent human response. That which might be destroyed may after all merit destruction. (The nihilistic method need not of course consist of bombs, especially since those are the means so often favored as well as controlled by those posing as anti-nihilists.) Other objections to nihilism include that it encourages too much logicality in trying to live by the inconvenient conclusion that most of our authorities, institutions and reasons may be false. We can readily tar nihilists with the blackness of consistency when the overwhelming evidence suggests that life mostly consists of a rainbowed muddle, though usually of very muddy colors. There stand also all sorts of selfish, lazy, predatory, sick, accommodating and other quite useful justifications for rejecting the nihilistic view that most of our accepted meanings are false and the society, if not the cosmos, a moral joke.

But nihilism, too, must be a practical choice. As the philosopher quoted above also notes, historically "the artist or intellectual does not assume the posture of nihilism . . . except in response to, and as a defense against, popular or global nihilism."[12] What we call a nihilistic view can be, and seems often historically to be, a sensitive and thoughtful response to the implicit nihilism of the political or cultural or even physical ordering of the world. Currently, men of the best will and wisdom analyze our conditions—from aggressively imperialistic nuclear powers through extreme technological destruction of the culture and environment to a fantastically accelerating over-population—as making vast, if not total, human destruction highly probable in the foreseeable future. A nihilistic attitude towards such orderings and their justifications seems a pertinent response, and has been for some time. Twentieth century nihil-

12Rosen, p. 232. (Rosen, rather than discussing these matters on which I quote him, uses them as excuses for presenting other philosophical arguments.) Or, as Norman Mailer cogently puts it: "nihilism might be the only answer to totalitarianism." *Armies of the Night* (New York, 1968), p. 199.

ists may generally be understood as countering the lack of values in irrational technocracy or mass totalitarianism or hypocritical liberalism, or whatever other social, political, and cultural descriptions one prefers for the age. Similarly, nineteenth century nihilists may generally be related to countering predatory industrialism or class autocracy or hypocritical Christianity, or whatever social, political, and cultural descriptions one prefers for that age. Nihilisms should be recognized as paradoxically positive in their counter-responses to the forces of annihilation.

Perhaps the most curious objection to nihilism is that it is not very destructive. No suicidal nihilists such as Melville's or even, say, Dostoyevsky's political nihilists in *The Possessed,* can be blamed for a destructiveness of major proportions, any more than can the youth rebellions or older radical criticisms denounced as our contemporary nihilisms. From our literature, we can see dramatic evidence that the more extreme the nihilistic view, the more self-limiting and even cathartic it often seems to be. That also suggests some discriminations between nihilisms. Bartleby's nihilistic resistance, I argued, stands far more heroic than the innocence of Billy Budd and the renunciation of Benito Cereno, though all three are suicidal. In distinguishing between those views and actions informed by the spirit of utter negation, we should recognize some as far more creative than others. Modern positivism, mysticism, and existentialism all insist on a dialectic of denial and a central nothingness, yet we would not likely conclude that they produce the same appeals and effects. I suggest that the nihilistic literary tradition of the past century has been of a positive cast and, as one existentialist put it, "a creative nihilism which points to the dark abyss of nothingness in order to warn and to rescue."[13] Instead of rejecting all recognizable nihilisms, and then ending up accepting that imbedded in things as they are, we might better choose the best nihilisms.

The objection to any particular nihilistic literary-philosophi-

[13]Emmanuel Mournier, quoted in Kurt Reinhardt, *The Existential Revolt* (New York, 1957), p. 2.

cal view, or even to any avowed nihilistic moral or political movement, cannot reasonably be in terms of its historical destructiveness. Comparison of nihilism with views and movements which claim the most elaborately positive values will hardly support such arguments. Objections to nihilism can hardly be understood separate from their emotional thrust. Not just disturbance and disequilibrium in those who have emotionally overinvested in bad institutions and false legitimizations and arbitrary meanings, but a rage against blasphemy, a horror at desanctification, must be recognized in anti-nihilisms. Only thus can we explain some of the outraged responses to existentialism or Dadaism or "revolution for the hell of it," or the view of a classic American author as essentially a nihilist. The antagonist relation of modernist culture to the bourgeois society takes its forms neither from class conflicts nor from cultural alternatives so much as it does from a religious psychodrama.

Put another way, nihilism seems to be to moral and cultural authority what anarchism is to social and political authority. We might further the intimate relation by applying to nihilism a current philosophical defense of anarchism.

The myth of legitimate authority is the secular reincarnation of that religious superstition which has finally ceased to play a significant role in the affairs of men. Like Christianity, the worship of the state has its fundamentalists, its revisionists, its ecumenicists . . . and its theological rationale. The philosophical anarchist is the atheist of politics . . . the belief in legitimacy, like the penchant for transcendent metaphysics, is an ineradicable irrationality of the human experience. However, the slow extinction of religious faith over the past two centuries may encourage us to hope that in time anarchism, like atheism, will become the accepted conviction of enlightened and rational men.[14]

14Robert Paul Wolff, "On Violence," *Journal of Philosophy*, LXVI (Oct. 2, 1969), p. 616. For a more modest defense of the anarchist valuation, see Kingsley Widmer, "On Refusing: Personal Preface to a Handbook on Selective Trouble-Making," *Anarchy* (London), IX (October, 1969), 289-300.

Charmingly put, but even an anarchist must suspect this philosopher of an overly optimistic rationalism. Is this what our other philosopher meant by his fear of "hope" in the nihilistic view? Such a sensitive and sensible hopefulness should certainly not be scorned. But the most powerful evidence for the existence of evil is secularized man's continuing proclivity for viciously irrelevant burdens, for guiltily carrying on cultural and political legitimacy and authority.

Intellectual nihilism might be seen as an emphatic extension of skepticism in the same way as atheism propounds a stronger assertion of agnosticism. No doubt matters of temperament, such as anger and courage, partly determine whether or not the agnostic skeptic will follow out his commitment to atheistic nihilism, but external conditions may also considerably influence the difference in degree. If we can lay down any laws for social and cultural change, then the first one I would propose would concern the drastic disproportions, the tragic disparities, between need and response, effort and result. The terrible frustrations that beset most efforts to make sensitive and sensible changes quite rightly drive good people into despair. Of course they then bitterly reject moderate rationalism and mild benevolence—the harshness which characterizes most intellectual formulations of nihilism—and arrive at the conclusion that nothing less than extremity will do.[15]

Nihilists, then, are forced to arrive at some such law of social and cultural change as this: Thou must negate much and demand much to achieve anything at all. (The second law of change might well be: Thou shalt not get what was tried for and hoped for but something much different.) Nihilism is dialectical, oppositional, countering—not an attitude in itself. It holds that nega-

[15]Anyone seriously engaged in dissent or protest or any effort at real institutional change knows by his nerve ends what I mean. Unlike most commentators, I would not confine this frustration to the present, though granting special contemporary difficulties. But see, for example, what happened to the antinomians, even as presented with the patient restraint of G. H. Williams, *The Radical Reformation* (Boston, 1952).

tion is utterly essential to even any possibility of meaning. With-out nihilism, whatever its guise, there could hardly be a serious dialectic of human values.

Two charitable qualifications might be added. Hopefully, nihilism can best take on its essential task in intellectual rather than physical destruction, in, as William Blake's lovely contraries have it, "Mental War" rather than "Corporeal War."[16] The trou-ble is, the anti-nihilists rarely fight fair. Then, too, the essential nihilist insights usually seem to require a special, alienating, kind of experience. To cite from a recent and generally quite ordi-nary account of a murderer reflecting on what he learned from his years of suffering: "I have learned in prison only three things: compassion for others, which perhaps makes the whole [sentence] worth while, a deep-rooted contempt for authority, and a recog-nition of my own inadequacies. . . ."[17] Part of the "inadequacy" of this ex-con was a sense of how little one could do to carry out the compassion and revolt, and therefore a conscious withdrawal from much of life, a full immediacy of denial approaching that of Melville's nihilistic characters.

The nihilistic implications of Melville's fables, as I have inter-preted them, deny ameliorist possibilities. This essentially leaves us with the logic of "nothing less." Nothing less will save the innocent Billy Budds, and make just the Captain Veres, than the practical abolition of the eighteenth century British navy, and whatever goes with it. Nothing less than a full revolution will free Babo's blacks, and liberate Captains Cereno and Delano from moral manicheanism, and all that goes with it. Nothing less than the transformation of a whole mode of consciousness and lifestyle will save the Bartlebys from suicide, and the benevolent rationalists from bad faith, and much that goes with it in our civilization. Melville so constructed, so perceived, his moral

---

[16]For an exposition of this view of Blake, see Kingsley Widmer, *The Literary Rebel* (Carbondale, Ill., 1965), ch. 2. Many of the other arguments in that book are closely related to those pursued here.

[17]Zeno [pseud.], *Life* (New York, 1968), p. 190.

situations that no alternate choice, no mere reform of an institution or redemption of a moral flaw, would answer the fated annihilations. These stories rightly terrify because of what we would have to choose to go beyond such nihilism.

Put more generally, the nihilistic "nothing less" provides quite a range of insights. It allows one to perceive, for example, radical necessity, such as that freedom and equality do not arise in an exploitative and repressive order from bland ameliorations or that false gods will not be smashed into dust by skeptical frowns. Ambivalences, of course, riddle what Melville called "this world of lies." Perhaps the most crucial of them can be seen in the antinihilists who insist on the forms and appearances of things—Melville's captains of this world—who turn out to do so because they believe in nothing else, and therefore are the total nihilists beyond whom one must go.

The more sincere nihilists, as Melville shows in his suicidal and blessed boys such as Bartleby, Billy, Benito, and Babo, do not exempt themselves from annihilation. A nihilist's near-paranoid despairs and rages, and his deficiencies in patience and balance and shrewdness and obtuseness, may be readily evident, though perhaps too easily noted by others. That the accelerating disenchantment became almost normative in modernist culture should not obscure for us that the negative and blasphemous responses are germane to much, indeed to the whole, of the history of Western culture. Perhaps it is only the collapse of our mythologies, and their basis in vital community, that makes the despair so self-conscious and clear. The nihilism of a Melville and the literature that followed him may be more easily acknowledged but is certainly no more intense than that of a Shakespeare or Rochester. However, for a century or so nihilism has served as the main secular heresy of our culture. Most of those we recognize as the major intellectual artists in the period carry the "great refusal" and "ultimate despair."

The exacerbation of nihilism represents absolutist responses to our systematic de-meaning of society, nature and life. Nihilistic responses seem to have been enlarged by the negative dialectical relation to the dominant "liberalism" and "one-dimensional civilization," assuming these to be partly distinguishable. Much of what I have previously described as the "benevolent rationalism" which Melville undercuts could be put with the historically shifting banners of liberalism. Melville treats that liberalism sympathetically (after all, he gets inside it) but with an obsessive irony. That benevolent rationalizing is not to be easily dismissed—hence the ambiguities of irony—because it provides our most decent efforts to carry past morality and authority into the present, to reasonably and prudently relate previous humaneness to cataclysmically transforming conditions—revolutions, massive manipulations of man and nature, the death of the gods. But such liberal impetus must, in its moderation and adaptability, appear the most immediate and outrageous falsity to the nihilist awareness. The good liberal would make legitimate, civilized, acceptable that which seems instead to require the most drastic negation. So we dramatically see in the otherwise very different novels of a Turgenev and a Dostoyevsky and a Melville. The liberal is most alien to the nihilist. Similar antagonisms play a major role in the philosophical polemics of an otherwise quite different Nietzsche and Heidegger and Sartre. The antithesis recurs with each of the major leaps of modernist culture: each transformation—realism, naturalism, impressionism, symbolism, expressionism, dadaism, surrealism, etc.—went to exasperated war with the reigning liberal civility and culture. And each time the nihilistic defiance seems to have lost by winning.

Much in the modern Western world can be characterized not only by the meaninglessness of its claims to legitimacy but by its pervasive and hypocritical imperative to denude all cosmic and communal order. It can simultaneously be released and disguised by taking on the drunkenness we call high culture. A nasty child among the liberal courtiers, the nihilist insists on the nakedness of our whole imperium. Enchanted as well as threatened, the fatuous courtiers turn the negations into an intoxicating game. As release and reenforcement, culture becomes the ultimate conspiracy and passivity-inducing "high" to maintain what annihilatingly is.

The nihilist finds himself entrapped in irrationality ornately rationalized. Our orderings remain so disparate from the material and human possibilities, our society and culture so absurd, that the only appropriate response beyond despair, "the imperative of the current situation," is "to become more negative and more utopian in opposition to the status quo."[18] For the nihilism of the century reacts to a fundamental processing in which all values become so manipulative and neutralized, so non-dimensional in the justification of the false and the evil, that one must demand the most drastic countering. Modern political systems and social institutions and cultural forms achieve an unprecedented self-perpetuation and self-rationalization that seems quite impervious to decent human reason and imagination. Those who now recognize that about the twentieth century should proportionately extend it back into the nineteenth. Thus I have used that classic American author of the past century as exemplary of the issue, of the conditions which demand and need nihilism.

The conventional liberal charge against the literature of nihilistic rage is that such works "lead to nothing" and illustrate "no yearning for good."[19] Contrary to rather commonsensical evidence, that assumes no progression in rejection and no utility in negation, and that the good can not take form through mock-

[18]Herbert Marcuse, *Negations* (Boston, 1968), p. XX. My language on several points here is, of course, indebted to *One-Dimensional Man* (Boston, 1964). In fairness I should add that Marcuse personally rejects associating his arguments with nihilism. See my "Marcuse's Allegory," *Nation*, 210 (June, 1970).

[19]The point was characteristically made by Irving Howe, *A World More Attractive* (New York, 1967) in discussing Céline. For a rebuttal and rather different emphasis, see Kingsley Widmer, "The Way Down to Wisdom of Louis-Ferdinand Céline," *Minnesota Review*, VIII (Winter 1968). See also my discussion of buffoonish nihilism as affirmation in a contemporary American writer. K. Widmer, *Henry Miller* (New York, 1963).

ery and revulsion and anger. What kind of yearning for goodness is it that does not passionately respond against the world we live in? What we call liberalism more and more desperately reveals that it is the main conservativism around.

Granted, the attacks on nihilism come also from others than conservative liberals. Even one of the most ardent defenders of modernism in art came, in his last published statement, to the conclusion that nihilism was overwhelming our culture: "Contemporary nihilism in art is simply a denial of art itself, a rejection of its social function. [Our art is now] characterized by incoherence, insensibility, brutality and ironic detachment. What we [should now] seek is 'a renaissance beyond the limits of nihilism'."[20] I have suggested that such a going beyond is already implicit in nihilistic art's own break with the usual limits, its carrying a drastic hope and freedom, and its demand for a transcendence of the present.

But, I hopefully suspect, what now looks like nihilism in the culture resides in something yet newer. Modernism, and both its intellectual nihilism and co-optative adaptation, may be on the way to being superseded. A post-modernist culture, more kinesthetic and communal and directly belligerent, less intellectual and individual and dialectically negative, may be arising out of, and partly against, the old modernist culture.[21] This would be part of a new communal responsiveness, with a culture more immediate and humane. To it, our modernist art—as well as proto-modernists such as Melville—would only have the status

[20]Herbert Read, "The Limits of Permissiveness," *Resurgence* (London), II (July-Oct., 1969), p. 17.

[21]I have been exploring this argument in a number of current and forthcoming discussions of the "counter-culture." See, for examples, "The Thrust of the Underculture," *The Nation*, 207 (Dec. 31, 1968); "The Rebellious Culture," *West Coast Review* (Canada), II (Fall, 1968); a review-article on T. Roszak's *The Making of A Counter Culture*, *The Village Voice* (Oct. 31, 1969); "The Electric Aesthetic and the Short-Circuit Ethic of the Current Populist Culture," *Arts in Society*, XI (Spring, 1970); and others which propose a new lifestyle as the way beyond.

of "classics." Or is that way beyond nihilism only a nihilistic wishful thinking, a faith in freedom and hope?

The central experience, I find, in responding to the nihilistic is the yearning to go beyond it. Such art, including Melville's, demands to be overcome—not only in the literature itself but in the world it meditates upon. We should not, therefore, now really want to go too far beyond nihilism.

INDEX

18; weaknesses in, 26, 27, 27n; dramatic adaptation of, 43n; as political novel, 47-58; political opinions deleted, 51, 54.

"*Billy Budd* and the Articles of War," C. B. Ives, 33n.

Billy Budd: Opera in Four Acts, E. M. Forester, Eric Crozier, Benjamin Britten, 43n.

"*Billy Budd:* Testament of Resistance," Paul Withim, 22n.

"*Billy Budd:* Two Concepts of Nature," John B. Noone, Jr., 25n.

Blackham, H. J., *Six Existentialist Thinkers*, 61n.

Blacks, as ambiguous motif, 63-64; Delano's racism, 64-65; as "evil," 65-66; Melville's treatment of, 66-72; Melville's manichaeism, 73; Babo as hero, 89.

Bowen, Merlin, *The Long Encounter, Self and Experience in the Writings of Herman Melville*, 32n, 77n, 103n.

Call Me Ishmael, Charles Olson, 35n.

Calvinism, in Melville, 73.

Camus, Albert, on Melville, 12n; *The Rebel*, morality of nihilism, 127n, 128n.

Canady, Jr., Nicholas, *Melville and Authority*, on power and authority, 83n.

Cardwell, Guy, "Melville's Gray Story: Symbols and Meaning in *Benito Cereno*," 84n.

Carlyle, Thomas, affinity with Melville, 11, 98.

Chase, Richard, *The American Novel and Its Tradition*, Burke's philosophy in *Billy Budd*, 50n; *Herman Melville*, homoeroticism in *Billy Budd*, 25n, schizophrenia, in *Bartleby*, 112n.

Christianity, Melville on, 40, 79.

Claggart, John, homoerotic sadism of, 25n; as Satan, 27-29, "outside society," 48; as Babo, 89.

The Conflict of Generations, Lewis S. Feuer, nihilism and young rebels, 128n.

Counter-culture, 139, 139n.

Criticism, literary, 3n, 6-14.

Dadaism, 128, 133.

D'Avanzo, Mario L., "Melville's *Bartleby* and Carlyle," 124n.

Delano, Capt. Amasa, as authority, 7; as historical character, 76; as Vere, 89, 89n; as Bartleby's attorney, 119-120.

Dialectics and Nihilism, Joseph Heller, 127n.

Dickens, Charles, affinity to Melville, 11, 98, 108.

Dostoyevsky, Feodor Michailovich, Bartleby like anti-hero of, 92-93, 114, 121-125, 132, 137.

Dryden, Edgar A., *Melville's Thematics of Form*, 9n, 50n, 89n.

Dugan, James, *The Great Mutiny*, 54n.

Efron, Arthur, on academic literary criticism, 3n.

Emerson, Ralph Waldo, 11.

The Existential Revolt, Kurt Reinhardt, 132n.

Existentialism, a philosophy, 12; Melville's, 12-13, 14, 63; rejection of "warship world," 58; "dread," 59; Heidegger on, 60-61, 62; meaning of death, 86; in Tolstoy, 87-88, 89-90, 94; as a positive philosophy, 132, 132n; bourgeois rejection of, 133.

Fantasia of the Unconscious, D. H. Lawrence, on nihilism, 128, 128n.

"Father-god problem," in Melville's life, 35-36.

Fathers and Sons, Ivan Turgenev, nihilism in, 127, 127n.

Fear and Trembling, Soren Kierkegaard, 35, 35n.

legalistic mind, 107, 118-119; in Melville's nihilism, 128.

Isolation, human, recurrent pattern of, in Melville, 6-7.

Ives, C. B., "*Billy Budd* and the Articles of War," 33*n*.

Jacobin revolutionism, in *Billy Budd*, 16.

James, William, *Naval History of Great Britain*, 54*n*.

Job, Bartleby's attorney as, 117*n*.

Jonas, Hans, *The Phenomenon of Life*, nihilism and gnosticism, 130*n*.

Kafka, Franz, similarities in *Bartleby*, 95*n*.

Kierkegaard, Soren, *Fear and Trembling*, 35, 35*n*; 61*n*.

"Lasting Institutions," a political ultimate, 20; Melville's mockery of, 47; Vere, supporter of, 48, 56; philosophy of, untenable, 49-50, 56, 57, hypocracy of, 57; *Billy Budd* undercuts, 58.

Lawrence, D. H., *Fantasia of the Unconscious*, on nihilism, 128, 128*n*.

Ledbetter, Kenneth, "The Ambiguity of *Billy Budd*," 24*n*.

Levin, Harry, *The Power of Blackness*, 53*n*, 78*n*, 101*n*.

Lewis, R. W. B., *The American Adam*, 27*n*. *Trials of the Word*, on slavery, 73*n*; on "dead letters," 120*n*.

Leyda, Jay, "Notes on Sources," on source figures for Bartleby, 96*n*.

Life, Zeno (pseud.), a nihilist's account, 135, 135*n*.

"The Limits of Permissiveness," Herbert Read, nihilism—a denial of art, 139, 193*n*.

The Long Encounter, Self and Experience in the Writings of Herman Melville, Merlin Bowen, 32*n*, 77*n*, 103*n*.

Love and Death in the American Novel, Leslie Fiedler, 53*n*, 64*n*.

Manicheanism, basis of *Benito Cereno*, 73-75; malignancy of, 89; 135.

Marcuse, Herbert, *Negations*, 138, 138*n*.

Marriage, Melville's disillusionment with, 77.

Marx, Leo, "Melville's Parable of the Walls," allegory in *Bartleby*, 99.

Matthiessen, F. O., *American Renaissance*, 11*n*.

"Meaning and Structure in *Bartleby*," Marvin Felheim, 104*n*.

Melville, Herman, little biographical material on, 10; relationships with Hawthorne and Emerson, 11; relationship to Carlyle, Dickens, Schopenhauer, 11-12; as anti-mythic post-romanticist, 12; as existentialist, 12-13, 63; Camus on, 12*n*; nihilism of, 14, 126-137; as political conservative, 50, 50*n*; political opinions deleted, 51-52; protester in *White Jacket*, 52*n*; mutiny justified in *Moby Dick*, 52-53; as historical moralizer, 54; on bigotry, 64-65, 69*n*; the black as heroic, 66-70; as racist, 70-75; Calvinism of, 73-74; glorification of masculine sailor's world, 77; use of allegory, 84-85 (see also Allegory); defender of stoicism, 93; as Bartleby, 99-193; influence of *Bleak House*, 108; similarity with Dostoyevsky, 114.

Melville and Authority, Nicholas Canaday, Jr., 83*n*.

"Melville and the Manichean Illusion," J. E. Oates, 58*n*.

"Melville and the Spurious Truth of Legalism," Charles Mitchell, 107*n*.

"Melville and Transcendentalism," Perry Miller, 11*n*.

"Melville the Scrivener," Stanley Edgar Hyman, 4*n*.

"Melville's *Bartleby* and Carlyle," Mario L. D'Avanzo, 124*n*.

Melville's Billy Budd and the Critics, a collection, 21*n*.